CLARE WINSTANLEY: TESTIMONIALS FROM STUDENTS

'Clare single-handedly helped me to improve my grades from an average of 50% to over 70% every single time. I have always struggled with essay writing for as long as I can remember. For my very first assignment I got 40% (just!) and this is when I approached the university for some academic help. I was matched with Clare, and she helped me to restructure my sentences, to reference correctly, and to improve my use of punctuation. For my second assignment I achieved 80% – all thanks to Clare! Throughout the next two years, I was consistently achieving 70%+. Clare was the best tutor I could have asked for!'

Jessica L. (BMus [Hons] – 1st Class)

'During my degree, Clare helped me improve my writing skills; we focused specifically on punctuation as this has always been my weakest area. Through our three years working together, both my ability and my confidence grew noticeably. I am, and always will be, incredibly grateful to Clare for working with me, and finding the most effective way for me to learn and improve.'

Bridget L. (BA [Hons] Costume with Textiles – 1st Class)

'Clare was fantastic! She not only provided me with practical support that I could apply to any writing scenario (e.g., she taught me the difference between "affect" / "effect" and "which" / "that"!), but she also gifted me with emotional support and empathy to my disability that only a truly talented tutor could provide in such a way.'

Lotti J. (MA Education [Internationalisation] – 1st Class)

'Clare guided me through the more challenging aspects of my law studies, especially in areas where I lacked confidence, such as proper punctuation. Diagnosed with dyslexia at an early age, I have received support throughout my education, but Clare was the only individual I worked with who fully understood the dyslexic brain. She recognised that rules were particularly helpful for dyslexics and especially for me. Clare took the time to explain and repeat the rules, ensuring I fully understood their application. I still follow her tips, such as determining comma and full stop placement by taking a breath in a sentence and avoiding starting sentences with present participles. Her support and expertise made a significant difference in my learning experience. Most importantly, I now feel confident in my communication skills, which have equipped me with the necessary tools to pursue a career in law.'

Teri S. (LLB – 2:1)

'Clare's guidance has significantly enhanced my spelling, punctuation, and grammar, boosting my confidence in writing and proofreading essays. Her book, a cornerstone for neurodivergent learners, is an essential tool for every writer. Thanks to her strategies, I now make fewer mistakes, and her lessons have become second nature.'

Anisa A. (MPharm – 2:1)

'Clare has been a lifeline throughout my long academic journey at Huddersfield University, from my Bachelor's degree through to my PhD. Her skills and tips around punctuation and grammar have enabled me to develop my own skills to the highest standard. Clare has also always brought fun to learning, which has made it so much easier. I now feel equipped with the tools to articulate, not just in my research but in all areas of my life, which is invaluable. Thank you, Clare.'

Stephanie T. (PhD Psychology)

'It has been a fantastic opportunity to work on some of the pages within this book. The pages were complex enough to stretch and challenge my learning, yet easy enough for someone with Dyslexia to understand. It has been a pleasure to work with the author of this book, who has such a great understanding of punctuation and grammar, yet is considerate and sympathetic to the needs of the learner.'

Cheryl H-F. (BA [Hons] Childhood Studies – 1st Class)

'I used to write very lengthy sentences and paragraphs, but shortening them by pruning and using commas and colons helps me to communicate more clearly; it's a technique Clare taught me and I continue to use in emails and reports.'

Will S. (BA [Hons] Marketing – 1st Class)

'During my time at Huddersfield University, Clare was my dyslexia tutor. She helped me greatly and was the catalyst that enabled me to achieve my first-class degree. She is helpful, knowledgeable, and the kind of character who goes above and beyond for her students, and went above and beyond for me when I needed her at one of the most stressful times of my studying life. I saw Clare once a week, and every time I saw her, she would teach me something new about grammar or sentence structure, but she gave me the life skills I needed in order to apply this in my future job. I believe a teacher teaches their students in order for them to successfully do it on their own, and this is exactly what Clare did during my time with her. Thank you, Clare, for all of your support and I am sincerely grateful for being paired with you.'

Claudia C. (BMus [Hons] – 1st Class)

'Clare had a massive impact on my degree result, moving my writing from 52-55 (mid 2:2) to 66-68 (high 2:1). The skills Clare taught me also helped to secure my postgraduate degree in Education. Clare helped me with all aspects of grammar, recognising and editing issues with sentence structure, and finally using semicolons correctly! I now 13 years later work as a primary school teacher and regularly teach the editing skills Clare taught me to the children I work with, as her techniques work so well!'

Michelle A. (BMus [Hons] – 2:1)

To Anisa,
with many thanks for your lovely testimonial and with warmest good wishes from
Clare

Clare Winstanley

Punctuation Matters!

A practical, proofreading guide for students

AUSTIN MACAULEY PUBLISHERS®
LONDON • CAMBRIDGE • NEW YORK • SHARJAH

Copyright © Clare Winstanley 2024

The right of Clare Winstanley to be identified as author of this work has been asserted by the author in accordance with sections 77 and 78 of the Copyright, Designs and Patents Act 1988.

All rights reserved. No part of this publication may be reproduced, stored in a retrieval system, or transmitted in any form or by any means, electronic, mechanical, photocopying, recording, or otherwise, without the prior permission of the publishers.

Any person who commits any unauthorised act in relation to this publication may be liable to criminal prosecution and civil claims for damages.

A CIP catalogue record for this title is available from the British Library.

ISBN 9781398476486 (Paperback)
ISBN 9781398476493 (ePub e-book)

www.austinmacauley.com

First Published 2024
Austin Macauley Publishers Ltd®
1 Canada Square
Canary Wharf
London
E14 5AA

This book is dedicated to

my beautiful and treasured granddaughters,
Phoebe and Maisie,
who bring our family so much joy

and to Mike, the love of my later life,
without whose encouragement and support
this book would never have been completed
and with thanks for twelve years of love, laughter, and dance.

A thousand thanks are due to the many university students with whom I have worked over the last 12 years, and who have patiently put up with me teaching them proofreading skills. I especially want to acknowledge and thank those who very kindly allowed me to adapt their work for this publication and/or trialled the teaching pages and chapters:

Amelia Fox	Claire Holgate	Matthew Jackson
Amy Templeman	Elizabeth Quinn	Matthew Lathlean
Anisa Azhar	Hannah Wood	Mollie Arnold-Jones
Anya Mistry	Helen Wilkinson	Natalie Reid
Ben Waudby	Jessica Lindsay	Nicole Swales
Bridget Lusk	Josh Brier	Tamsin Winstanley
Cath Jones	Lauren Donaghey	Teri Sutton
Charis Sykes	Lauren Hampson	Terri Ledger
Cheryl Houghton-Smith	Lauren Saint Hilaire	
Chloe Hewitt	Lotti Johnson	

I am also indebted to Peter Mayall for reviewing the manuscript and for his helpful comments on teaching the possessive apostrophe.

Finally, I would like to thank Sogand Seydjoo Bashman for her beautiful cover design and Norman Drax for his delightful illustrations.

CONTENTS

Introduction 11

Proofreading Exercises 13

    Proofreading Exercise 1 14

    Proofreading Exercise 2 22

    Proofreading Exercise 3 30

    Proofreading Exercise 5 46

    Proofreading Exercise 6 54

    Proofreading Exercise 7 62

    Proofreading Exercise 8 70

    Proofreading Exercise 9 78

    Proofreading Exercise 10 88

Teaching Pages 99

    A and the – Indefinite and Definite Articles 100

    As and Has 103

    Abbreviations in References 106

    Agreement of Verbs 108

    Challenge 1 115

    Although 117

    Apostrophes 119

    Apostrophes in Contractions 124

    A Note About Letters and Dates: 125

    Been/Being 126

    Colons and Semicolons, Dots and Dashes 128

    Semicolons 130

    Dots and Dashes 134

    Commas 136

    First and Third Person 146

    Homophones and Similar-Sounding Words! 148

    Hyphens 162

    Introductory, Intermediate and Following Phrases 167

    Following Phrases 169

    Intermediate Phrases 172

    Parts of Speech 179

- Plurals 182
- Pruning Excess Words 185
- Rephrasing 191
- 'Th' and 'wh' Words 199
- While/Whilst 204
- Whereas 206
- Whether 208

Corrected versions 209

- A and An 210
- As and Has 210
- Agreement of Verbs 210
- Although 213
- Apostrophes – Inserted 213
- Been or Being – Inserted 215
- Colons and Semicolons – Inserted 216
- Commas – Inserted 218
- First and Third Person – Amended 219
- Hyphens – Inserted 219
- Introductory, Intermediate and Following Phrases – Corrected 222
- Excess Words Pruned 224
- 'Th' and 'wh' Words 226
- 20 Dos and Don'ts! 230

CONGRATULATIONS! 235

INTRODUCTION

In a lifetime of working with students, particularly in the last 12 years tutoring at a university, I have discovered that students find it difficult to proofread their own work or give up, feeling unable to do so. I empathise! Whether I dash off a letter of complaint or take the time to craft an article, I may think I have proofread it carefully, but you can bet your bottom dollar my partner will spot something I have missed if he reads it through! Why is that? Well, when we are expressing ourselves in writing, we invest ourselves in what we are writing and may well be carried away by the emotion involved, the need to meet an imminent deadline, or simply be using all our mental energy just to transfer our thoughts to paper. That is why, when we have finished the work, we need to step back and examine it more critically – to proofread it.

So, what are we looking for? How do we know what is acceptable or grammatically correct unless we have some guidelines to follow? From talking with my students, I know that either they were not taught grammar when they were at school (such an old-fashioned concept!), or that they have forgotten what they were taught in the packed National Curriculum of their youth, when in each week of every term they had to learn a certain amount of phonics and rules, with no time for consolidation, before the next section of the prescribed curriculum was upon them. What if they missed a week of school through illness? They would have missed those rules and snippets of wisdom! What then?

The university students I work with today want help planning, structuring and proofreading their assignments. Unfortunately, much as I would love to proofread their work for them, I cannot. University regulations indicate that if I make changes to a student's work it becomes <u>my</u> work, and they will be accused of plagiarism… Thus, I have spent the last 12 years teaching students how to develop and hone their <u>own</u> proofreading skills, and those skills have now been distilled into this guide – for you to apply and profit by!

As this is a guide for students, including those from other countries who grapple with the complexities of English grammar, I have avoided using complicated terms like 'subject modifiers' and 'subordinate clauses' in favour of simple phrases that are easier to grasp. Purists of the English language may not necessarily agree with my explanations, but the competence and confidence of my students have improved significantly, as their grades and testimonials attest, and that is what matters most to me.

How to Use This Book

The book is divided into two halves. The first half contains ten chapters, each containing an example of a student's work for you to proofread. It is so much easier to proofread someone else's work, because you are not emotionally invested in it and don't mind defacing the work with a marker's red pen, figuratively speaking! At the beginning of each chapter, my wise owl with big eyes will instruct you what to look out for, and each paragraph will end with the number of errors to be found. Please don't worry if you can't find all the errors! In fact, it would be good NOT to find them all, as you will learn more from discovering the ones you missed.

Following the example for you to proofread, you will see a bright idea to make your writing more academic, and a scholarly word to look up if you do not know it and with which you can enhance your writing. Then you will find the proofread version of the text with all changes tracked, against which you can compare your own version and see how many of the errors you found. You can record the number of errors you found on the Reflections page, where you are encouraged to reflect on what you have learnt from the exercise. You may like to repeat the proofreading exercise again in a few weeks to see if you improve your score! Additionally, there are tips in the margin to help you understand certain errors and you will be directed to a teaching page in the second half of the book for further help, should you wish to access it.

Any references used in the chapters are listed at the bottom of the third section of each chapter, which is a corrected version of the original text. References follow APA 7th guidelines. Where they differ from Harvard, this will be noted.

Just as a squirrel stores nuts to sustain it through the winter, you can squirrel away nuggets from this proofreading guide to sustain you in your writing for life! The teaching pages contain a wealth of enlightening sections, including pruning and rephrasing work, punctuation, abbreviations, homophones (there/their etc.), and many more, to consolidate your learning from the proofreading exercises. There are examples to practise and challenges to attempt! You can compare your answers with those in the 'Corrected versions' section at the back of the book and dip into the 20 Dos and Don'ts to discover some valuable extra tips! You will then graduate as a competent proofreader!

PROOFREADING EXERCISES

Proofreading Exercise 1

Proofread the following exercise, correcting it and adding punctuation where necessary. Note that not every sentence contains an error. Then compare your version with the corrected one in the next section.

You may like to use an acetate sheet with a drywipe marker pen or some tracing paper on which to mark your errors, so that you can repeat the proofreading exercises at a later date and see how much you have learnt!

Practise the use of commas and hyphens.

- Commas separate a name from a detail.
- They also separate multiple adjectives.
- Commas can be used instead of brackets. However, in the last sentence of paragraph 3, it would be helpful to use brackets to separate the 'definitions' from the terms, to make the sentence easier to read.
- Hyphens are used to join two or three words that are combined to make one adjective or noun e.g., second-hand clothes and mother-in-law.
- Ages from one to nine are written as words. Numerals are used for ages from 10. ?-year-old would be hyphenated when followed by a noun.

The Background to the Harry Potter Books

The Harry Potter series consist of seven books that have been adapted into eight films. The series follows the life of Harry Potter a wizard, and starts with 11 year old Harry living with his muggle (non-magic) aunt uncle and cousin (Rowling 1997). Harry discovers he is a wizard when he is invited to attend Hogwarts School of Witchcraft and Wizardry (Rowling, 1997). Alongside his new friends Hermione Granger and Ronald Weasley Harry Potter fights against his enemy Lord Voldemort – 'He Who Must Not Be Named. **10 errors**

Harry finds out Lord Voldemort killed his parent when he was one year old. Due to Harry's mother's strong love shielding Harry Voldemort's spell rebounded on him. Harry was left with a lightning-shaped scar on his forehead. However because Voldemort created horcruxes to preserve his soul allowing him to keep living Harry faces Voldemort several times throughout the series before finally defeating him at the Battle of Hogwarts (Rowling 2007). **7 errors**

The novels are based in a parallel world to the one we know. The story is simply good versus evil. As Harry grows throughout the series he becomes a brave strong character who faces Voldemort a cruel and evil character who believes power should be given to 'pure-bloods'. Pure-bloods are wizards who are born into wizard-only families. Voldemort does not want half bloods half wizard, half muggle and muggle borns wizards with muggle parents to exist. **10 errors**

14

The wizarding world of Harry Potter continues to expand every day, with more films being produced such as the Fantastic Beasts and Where to Find Them series, which is based on the schoolbooks Harry studies at Hogwarts (Rowling, 2001). J. K. Rowling also wrote a screenplay Harry Potter and the Cursed Child (2016) which is now in theatre.

3 errors

Dictionary Corner

proliferate

If you don't know this word, use your dictionary, phone or Google to find the meaning of **proliferate** and consider using it in your writing!

Bright ideas to make your writing more academic

Know when to use inverted commas or italics for titles:

Italics are used for the titles of complete works – books, plays and newspapers. Inverted commas are used for short works, like chapters, poems, articles or short stories. Thus, 'The Boy Who Lived' is the first chapter of *Harry Potter and the Philosopher's Stone*.

Find the three titles in the proofreading exercise above and change them into italics.

Quotation marks are used in pairs to introduce speech or quotations.

Proofreading Exercise 1 – Corrected

Compare your corrected version with the one below. The small raised numbers show where the corrections are: the numbers in pink indicate notes in the margin. (General notes are marked with small letters in pink.) Count how many errors you corrected and write your score on the 'Reflections' page overleaf.

The Background to the Harry Potter Books

Paragraph 1

1. Although 'series' looks as though it is plural, it is in fact a singular noun so needs a singular verb – consists. See the teaching pages on 'Agreement of verbs' (from page 108).

2. Here, the comma replaces the words "who is".

7. Here, the comma replaces the words "who are".

Paragraph 2

a. This does not need to be hyphenated because it is not followed by a noun, as in 'a one-year-old puppy'.

b. This is a complex sentence that needs commas to divide its various components – the introductory word, the proviso, the intermediate phrase, the thrust of the sentence and the following phrase. See the teaching pages on 'Introductory, intermediate and following phrases' (from page 167).

Paragraph 3

c. You could simply use commas instead of brackets for the explanations, but using brackets makes it clear that Voldemort does not want these two specific groups (half-bloods and muggle-borns) to exist. Otherwise, it could be construed there are 5 groups of people he wished did not exist.

The *Harry Potter* series consist**s**[1] of seven books that have been adapted into eight films. The series follows the life of Harry Potter**,**[2] a wizard, and starts with 11**-**[3]year**-**[4]old Harry living with his muggle (non-magic) aunt**,**[5] uncle and cousin (Rowling**,**[6] 1997). Harry discovers he is a wizard when he is invited to attend Hogwarts School of Witchcraft and Wizardry (Rowling, 1997). Alongside his new friends**,**[7] Hermione Granger and Ronald Weasley**,**[8] Harry Potter fights against his enemy**,**[9] Lord Voldemort - 'He Who Must Not Be Named**'**[10]. **10 errors**

Harry finds out Lord Voldemort killed his parent**s**[1] when he was one year old.[a] Due to Harry's mother's strong love shielding Harry**,**[2] Voldemort's spell rebounded on him. Harry was left with a lightning-shaped scar on his forehead. However**,**[3] because Voldemort created horcruxes to preserve his soul**,**[4] allowing him to keep living**,**[5] Harry faces Voldemort several times throughout the series**,**[6] before finally defeating him at the Battle of Hogwarts (Rowling**,**[7] 2007).[b] **7 errors**

The novels are based in a parallel world to the one we know. The story is simply good versus evil. As Harry grows throughout the series**,**[1] he becomes a brave**,**[2] strong character who faces Voldemort**,**[3] a cruel and evil character**,**[4] who believes power should be given to 'pure-bloods'. Pure-bloods are wizards who are born into wizard-only families. Voldemort does not want half-bloods[5] (**[6]half wizard, half muggle)[7] and muggle-borns[8] ([9]wizards with muggle parents)[10] to exist.[c] **10 errors**

The wizarding world of Harry Potter continues to expand every day, with more films being produced,[1] such as the *Fantastic Beasts and Where to Find Them* series, which is based on the schoolbooks Harry studies at Hogwarts (Rowling, 2001). J. K. Rowling also wrote a screenplay,[2] *Harry Potter and the Cursed Child* (2016),[3] which is now in theatre. **3 errors**

Total: 30 errors

Space below for notes

Reflections

Be honest, as you should see how your score improves with each passage you proofread! Finally, reflect on what you have learnt from this piece.

1st Proofreading

Date: _____   Score: _____ /30

What two main points have I learnt?

1.

2.

2nd Proofreading

Date: _____   Score: _____ /30

How did I improve?

1.

2.

What do I still need to remember?

1.

2.

Please use this page for notes

Proofreading Exercise 1 – Final Version!

Although they look very different, this text is the same as the corrected version from page 16; the only difference is that the highlighted changes and explanatory notes have been removed. (This is also the case for all subsequent proofreading exercises.)

The Background to the Harry Potter Books

The *Harry Potter* series consists of seven books that have been adapted into eight films. The series follows the life of Harry Potter, a wizard, and starts with 11-year-old Harry living with his muggle (non-magic) aunt, uncle and cousin (Rowling, 1997). Harry discovers he is a wizard when he is invited to attend Hogwarts School of Witchcraft and Wizardry (Rowling, 1997). Alongside his new friends, Hermione Granger and Ronald Weasley, Harry Potter fights against his enemy, Lord Voldemort – 'He Who Must Not Be Named'.

Harry finds out Lord Voldemort killed his parents when he was one year old. Due to Harry's mother's strong love shielding Harry, Voldemort's spell rebounded on him. Harry was left with a lightning-shaped scar on his forehead. However, because Voldemort created horcruxes to preserve his soul, allowing him to keep living, Harry faces Voldemort several times throughout the series, before finally defeating him at the Battle of Hogwarts (Rowling, 2007).

The novels are based in a parallel world to the one we know. The story is simply good versus evil. As Harry grows throughout the series, he becomes a brave, strong character who faces Voldemort, a cruel and evil character, who believes power should be given to 'pure-bloods'. Pure-bloods are wizards who are born into wizard-only families. Voldemort does not want half-bloods (half wizard, half muggle) and muggle-borns (wizards with muggle parents) to exist.

The wizarding world of Harry Potter continues to expand every day with more films being produced, such as the *Fantastic Beasts and Where to Find Them* series (Rowling, 2001), which is based on the schoolbooks Harry studies at Hogwarts. J. K. Rowling also wrote a screenplay, *Harry Potter and the Cursed Child* (2016), which is now in theatre.

Adapted and used with the kind permission of the author, as indicated in the acknowledgements.

References as provided by the author:

Rowling, J. K. (1997). *Harry Potter and the Philosopher's Stone.* Bloomsbury Children's Books.

Rowling, J. K. (2001). *Fantastic Beasts and Where to Find Them.* Bloomsbury Children's Books.

Rowling, J. K. (2007). *Harry Potter and the Deathly Hallows: Part 2.* Bloomsbury Children's Books.

Rowling, J. K. (2016). *Harry Potter and the Cursed Child.* Little, Brown and Co.

Proofreading Exercise 2

Proofread the following exercise, correcting it and adding punctuation where necessary. Note that not every sentence contains an error. Then compare your version with the corrected one in the next section.

You may like to use an acetate sheet with a drywipe marker pen or some tracing paper on which to mark your errors, so that you can repeat the proofreading exercises at a later date and see how much you have learnt!

Use commas to:

- Separate a name from a detail
- Enclose phrases in the middle of sentences
- Introduce a quotation that is a full sentence
- Separate multiple adjectives (describing words)

There is a set of teaching pages on 'Commas' later in the book (from page 136).

Space below for notes

What does this document by the 12th century chronicler, Fulcher of Chartres, tell us about Pope Urban II's impact on the First Crusade?

Urban II speech at Clermont had a major impact in triggering a new kind of religious pilgrimage, in the form of the Crusades that spanned the ensuing two centurys. When referring to the affects of Urban II's speech at Clermont, Tyerman (2007) states "It has been seen as setting in train one of the most renowned sequence of events in Western Europe and Christianity." Therefor, the speech was the main course of the First Crusade which spurred Christians from across Europe led by noblemen like Raymond of Toulouse and Bohemond of Toronto to travel to the east to retake the holy cities. **9 errors**

In 1099 three years after the speech at Clermont the Crusaders captured the longed for city of Jerusalem. Phillips (2010) described the event as "an astonishing achievement". This is because of the lack of planning and the short amount of time from the speech to when the goal was achieved. The First Crusade served as a spur to other Christians encouraging many to build on their achievements by going on a Crusade. Consequently Urban's speech at Clermont had a major impact on the notion of Christian pilgrimage and the desired retaking of holy places. **5 errors**

One important aspect of the document is Urbans assertion that he posed the power of God to offer redemption to those Christians who went to fight in the Crusade. This is evident in the line "All who die by the way, whether by land or by sea, or in battle against the pagans, shall have immediate remission of sins. This I grant them through the power of God with which I am invested" (Fulcher of Chartres, cited in Peters, 1998). This is an important statement, as Urban is trying to assert his spiritual authority as Pope which was under threat from a fragmented Europe. Frankopan (2012) notes that it was "a time of violent dispute between the papacy and the leading magnates of Europe, which saw rulers being dramatically excommunicated". The most prominent of these was the dispute between his predecessor Pope Gregory VII and Henry IV the Holy Roman Emperor. Henry was excommunicated twice during his pontificate. **7 errors**

The significance of this is that Henry IV along with some of his bishops installed an opposing pope Pope Clement III. Clement was a serious threat to Urban II and the unity of the church. Thus, the document is important in showing us how Urban was trying to reistablish the importance of the church to the people by offering them the chance of redemption if they were to go on a Crusade. Baldwin & Setton (2016) remark that Urban was successful in "restoring to the papacy the prestige which Gregory had lost", impart because of the success that the speech at Clermont had in uniting Christians as a church, in the common goal of retaking the holy places. Therefore the document is important in inferring the motivations that Urban II had in promoting the first crusade.

9 errors

Dictionary Corner

refute

If you don't know this word, use your dictionary, phone or Google to find the meaning of **refute** and consider using it in your writing!

Bright ideas to make your writing more academic

Avoid using 'contractions', such as "there's", "isn't" or "aren't", where two words are contracted together to make one. There are numerous examples, and we use them a great deal in speech, but they should NOT feature in academic writing! Always use the full version – "there is", "is not" or "are not". A bonus of doing this is that you do not have to worry about inserting the apostrophe for the missing letter!

Also avoid writing, "This is because…" as in paragraph 2, line 3. You could simply replace the full stop at the end of the previous sentence with a comma, omit "This is" and continue from "because".

Don't worry about sentences being too long. Providing you have commas to allow you to breathe, it is perfectly acceptable to have some long sentences. Balance them with shorter ones for contrast.

Space below for notes

Proofreading Exercise 2 – Corrected

Compare your corrected version with the one below. The small raised numbers show where the corrections are: the numbers in pink indicate notes in the margin. Count how many errors you corrected and write your score on the 'Reflections' page overleaf.

Paragraph 1

3   See page 148 for help with this tricky homophone.

5   'Therefore' needs an 'e' and also a comma, as it is an introductory word that should be separate from the main sentence.

7   The sentence could end here, but you are adding more detail or an explanation. See the teaching pages on 'Commas' (from page 136), especially in front of 'as', 'because' and 'which'.

8   The sentence could read "…which spurred Christians from across Europe to travel to the east…" Therefore, I have put commas around the intermediate phrase, "led by noblemen like Raymond of Toulouse and Bohemond of Toronto", as though it was an aside or a detail in brackets.

Paragraph 2

3   Hyphenate two words that you put together to make one adjective (describing word). See 'Hyphens' on page 162.

4   The 'ing' verb suggests a following phrase that is separated from the main sentence by a comma. See 'Introductory, intermediate and following phrases' on page 167.

5   'Consequently' is an introductory word, so is separated from the main sentence by a comma.

Paragraph 3

1   The assertion 'belongs' to Urban, so we need the possessive apostrophe here. See the teaching pages on 'Apostrophes' from page 119.

4   See the teaching pages on 'Th' and 'wh' words from page 199.

What does this document by the 12th century chronicler, Fulcher of Chartres, tell us about Pope Urban II's impact on the First Crusade?

Urban II**'s**[1] speech at Clermont had a major impact in triggering a new kind of religious pilgrimage, in the form of the Crusades that spanned the ensuing two ~~centurys~~ **centuries**.[2] When referring to the ~~a~~effects[3] of Urban II's speech at Clermont, Tyerman (2007) states**,**[4] "It has been seen as setting in train one of the most renowned sequence of events in Western Europe and Christianity." Therefor**e**[5], the speech was the main ~~course~~ **cause**[6] of the First Crusade**,**[7] which spurred Christians from across Europe**,**[8] led by noblemen like Raymond of Toulouse and Bohemond of Toronto**,**[9] to travel to the east to retake the holy cities.   **9 errors**

In 1099**,**[1] three years after the speech at Clermont**,**[2] the Crusaders captured the longed**-**for[3] city of Jerusalem. Phillips (2010) described the event as "an astonishing achievement"~~. This is~~**,** because of the lack of planning and the short amount of time from the speech to when the goal was achieved. The First Crusade served as a spur to other Christians**,**[4] encouraging many to build on their achievements by going on a Crusade. Consequently**,**[5] Urban's speech at Clermont had a major impact on the notion of Christian pilgrimage and the desired retaking of holy places.   **5 errors**

One important aspect of the document is Urban**'**s[1] assertion that he pos**sess**ed[2] the power of God to offer redemption to those Christians who went to fight in the Crusade. This is evident in the line**,**[3] "All who die by the way, whether by land or by sea, or in battle against the pagans, shall have immediate remission of sins. This I grant them through the power of God with which I am invested" (Fulcher of Chartres, cited in Peters, 1998). This is an important statement, as Urban is trying to assert his spiritual authority as Pope**,**[4] which was under threat from a fragmented Europe.

Frankopan (2012) notes that it was "a time of violent dispute between the papacy and the leading magnates of Europe, which saw rulers being dramatically excommunicated". The most prominent of these was the dispute between his predecessor,[5] Pope Gregory VII,[6] and Henry IV,[7] the Holy Roman Emperor. Henry was excommunicated twice during his pontificate. **7 errors**

The significance of this is that Henry IV,[1] along with some of his bishops,[2] installed an opposing pope,[3] Pope Clement III. Clement was a serious threat to Urban II and the unity of the church. Thus, the document is important in showing us how Urban was trying to ~~reistablish~~ **re-establish**[4] the importance of the church to the people,[5] by offering them the chance of redemption if they were to go on a Crusade. Baldwin & Setton (2016) remark that Urban was successful in "restoring to the papacy the prestige which Gregory had lost", **in**[6] ~~im~~part because of the success that the speech at Clermont had in uniting Christians as a church, in the common goal of retaking the holy places. Therefore,[7] the document is important in inferring the motivations that Urban II had in promoting the F~~f~~irst[8] C~~c~~rusade[9]. **9 errors**

Total: 30 errors

Paragraph 4

4 Increasingly in English, hyphens are being dropped after prefixes like 're-', but 're-establish' is easier to read with a hyphen separating the two 'e's, which are pronounced differently. See the teaching pages on 'Hyphens' (from page 162).

5 Note the 'ing' verb, indicating a following phrase that follows a comma!

6 'In part' can sound like 'impart', but they have very different meanings. If you were struggling to meet the word count, you could change 'in part' to 'partly'.

8, 9 Keep your focus as you near the end of the text so that you don't miss errors!

Reflections

Be honest, as you should see how your score improves with each passage you proofread! Finally, reflect on what you have learnt from this piece.

1st Proofreading

Date: _____   Score: _____ /30

What two main points have I learnt?

1.

2.

2nd Proofreading

Date: _____   Score: _____ /30

How did I improve?

1.

2.

What do I still need to remember?

1.

2.

Please use this page for notes

Proofreading Exercise 2 – Final Version!

What does this document by the 12th century chronicler, Fulcher of Chartres, tell us about Pope Urban II's impact on the First Crusade?

Urban II's speech at Clermont had a major impact in triggering a new kind of religious pilgrimage, in the form of the Crusades that spanned the ensuing two centuries. When referring to the effects of Urban II's speech at Clermont, Tyerman (2007) states, "It has been seen as setting in train one of the most renowned sequence of events in Western Europe and Christianity." Therefore, the speech was the main cause of the First Crusade, which spurred Christians from across Europe, led by noblemen like Raymond of Toulouse and Bohemond of Toronto, to travel to the east to retake the holy cities.

In 1099, three years after the speech at Clermont, the Crusaders captured the longed-for city of Jerusalem. Phillips (2010) described the event as "an astonishing achievement", because of the lack of planning and the short amount of time from the speech to when the goal was achieved. The First Crusade served as a spur to other Christians, encouraging many to build on their achievements by going on a Crusade. Consequently, Urban's speech at Clermont had a major impact on the notion of Christian pilgrimage and the desired retaking of holy places.

One important aspect of the document is Urban's assertion that he possessed the power of God to offer redemption to those Christians who went to fight in the Crusade. This is evident in the line, "All who die by the way, whether by land or by sea, or in battle against the pagans, shall have immediate remission of sins. This I grant them through the power of God with which I am invested" (Fulcher of Chartres, cited in Peters, 1998). This is an important statement, as Urban is trying to assert his spiritual authority as Pope, which was under threat from a fragmented Europe. Frankopan

(2012) notes that it was "a time of violent dispute between the papacy and the leading magnates of Europe, which saw rulers being dramatically excommunicated". The most prominent of these was the dispute between his predecessor, Pope Gregory VII, and Henry IV, the Holy Roman Emperor. Henry was excommunicated twice during his pontificate.

The significance of this is that Henry IV, along with some of his bishops, installed an opposing pope, Pope Clement III. Clement was a serious threat to Urban II and the unity of the church. Thus, the document is important in showing us how Urban was trying to re-establish the importance of the church to the people, by offering them the chance of redemption if they were to go on a Crusade. Baldwin & Setton (2016) remark that Urban was successful in "restoring to the papacy the prestige which Gregory had lost", in part because of the success that the speech at Clermont had in uniting Christians as a church, in the common goal of retaking the holy places. Therefore, the document is important in inferring the motivations that Urban II had in promoting the First Crusade.

Adapted and used with the kind permission of the author, as indicated in the acknowledgements.

References as provided by the author:

Baldwin, M. W., & Setton, K. M. (2016). *A history of the crusades: Volume 1, the first hundred years.* Philadelphia, Pa: University of Pennsylvania Press.

Frankopan, P. (2012). *The first crusade: The call from the east.* Cambridge, MA: Harvard University Press.

Peters, E. (1998). *The First Crusade: "The Chronicle of Fulcher of Chartres" and Other Source Materials* (2nd ed.). Philadelphia, Pa: University of Philadelphia Press.

Phillips, J. P. (2010). *Holy Warriors: a modern history of the Crusades* (1st ed.). Vintage.

Tyerman, C. T. (2007). *God's war: a new history of the Crusades* (1st ed.). Penguin Group.

Proofreading Exercise 3

Proofread the following exercise, correcting it and adding punctuation where necessary. Note that not every sentence contains an error. Then compare your version with the corrected one in the next section.

> You may like to use an acetate sheet with a drywipe marker pen or some tracing paper on which to mark your errors, so that you can repeat the proofreading exercises at a later date and see how much you have learnt!
>
> In general, look out for missing apostrophes, commas, colons and semicolons.
>
> If you are unsure about any of these, check out the appropriate teaching pages.
>
> In particular, in the lower half of paragraph 3, look for a sentence where you could cut 2 words to make a smoother sentence that needs no comma.

Carlos Ghosn

Carlos Ghosn is a global buisness manager known for cutting costs in order to restore a firms profitability. His career started with the French tyre firm Michelin, he was involved with the restructuring of Michelin in North America. This essay will explore Carlos Ghosn's approach to global management using the pyramid model of leadership. **5 errors**

The pyramid model looks at the leadership capabilitys that a manger can develop and implement across cultures (Steers and Osland, 2019). The model is in the form of a pyramid to show that there is certain skills and competencies that need to be built upon. The levels also represent the progression of a leader (Mendenhall et al, 2008). The model consists of five levels, which from bottom to top are; Global business knowledge; threshold traits; multicultural competence; global management skills; and system skills (Steers & Osland, 2019) **8 errors**

Carlos Ghosn originally wanted to westernise Nissan. He did this by creating western-style multi-national and cross functional teams. He also introduced a western-style pay system this replaced the seniority pay system that had been deeply entrenched in Japanese culture. Showing that he lacked cultural intelligence. However Ghosn then showed that he was challenging Japanese cultural traditions to globalise Nissan. By creating a global firm it demonstrated Ghosn's ability to embrace cultural differences and include them in his organisational culture. **8 errors**

It is argued that leaders with global management skills are in high demand among employers as they enable the company to secure a competitive edge in the ever changing global marketplace (Hrehová, Svitačová & Klimková 2017). Ghosn's way of managing Nissan was different to his predecessor, but his new management style resulted in Nissan reporting record profits. A leader's interpersonal skills plays a vital role when building trust with there employees Terrell, (2018). Also, it is important that global leaders understand the concept of mindful communication (Steers & osland, 2019). This links with a leaders ability to empathise with their team, improving the quality of the relationships that are formed (Lange & Rowold, 2019). When a leader listens to and understands their followers, there is more likely to be successfull stress management within the team.

9 errors

Dictionary Corner

corroborate

If you don't know this word, use your dictionary, phone or Google to find the meaning of **corroborate** and consider using it in your writing!

Bright ideas to make your writing more academic

1. Take time to plan your essay/assignment. Mind maps are a great way to brainstorm ideas for your topic, using key words from the assignment brief and the learning objectives as triggers.

2. Once you have jotted down your ideas, you can begin to group them into points and put them in order. Your points can become your paragraphs. Research the topic and add more ideas and information to your mind map. Then when you begin to write, you will know what you are going to say, and your writing will be structured and will flow more easily.

3. Try to link your paragraphs so that your writing is cohesive. The essay above has a good example in paragraphs 1 and 2, where a concept is mentioned at the end of the first paragraph and explained in the second.

Proofreading Exercise 3 – Corrected

Compare your corrected version with the one below. The small raised numbers show where the corrections are: the numbers in pink indicate notes in the margin. Count how many errors you corrected and write your score on the 'Reflections' page overleaf.

Carlos Ghosn

Paragraph 1

2. The profitability 'belongs' to the firm, so you need the possessive apostrophe. See the teaching pages on 'Apostrophes' (from page 119).

4. There are two sentences here, so you EITHER need to join them with a link word like 'and' OR a sentence break is needed. You could use a full stop, but a semicolon would be better. See the teaching pages on 'Colons, semicolons, dots and dashes' (page 128).

a. The 'ing' verb suggests a following phrase, which you separate from the main sentence with a comma. See the teaching pages on 'Introductory, intermediate and following phrases' (from page 167).

Paragraph 2

1. See the teaching pages on 'Plurals' (from page 182).

3. Ampersands, rather than the word 'and', are used between two authors in parenthetical in-text citations in APA referencing. When used in a sentence, two authors would be linked by the word 'and'. In Harvard referencing 'and' links the two authors, instead of an ampersand.

5. It looks strange to have a full stop, followed by a comma. See the teaching pages on 'Abbreviations' for the explanation (from page 106).

6. A colon introduces a list. The semicolon separates items in the list.

7. A capital letter is not needed after a semicolon or a colon, unless what follows is a proper noun, like someone's name.

Carlos Ghosn is a global bu~~is~~**si**ness[1] manager known for cutting costs in order to restore a firm**'s**[2] profitability. His career started with the French tyre firm**,**[3] Michelin~~;~~**,**[4] he was involved with the restructuring of Michelin in North America. This essay will explore Carlos Ghosn's approach to global management**,**[5] using[a] the pyramid model of leadership.

5 errors

The pyramid model looks at the leadership ~~capabilitys~~ **capabilities**[1] that a man**a**ger[2] can develop and implement across cultures (Steers ~~and~~ **&**[3] Osland, 2019). The model is in the form of a pyramid to show that there ~~is~~ **are**[4] certain skills and competencies that need to be built upon. The levels also represent the progression of a leader (Mendenhall et al**.**,[5] 2008). The model consists of five levels, which from bottom to top are~~;~~**:**[6] ~~G~~**g**lobal[7] business knowledge; threshold traits; multicultural competence; global management skills; and system skills (Steers & Osland, 2019)**.**[8] **8 errors**

32

Carlos Ghosn originally wanted to westernise Nissan. He did this by creating western-style,[1] multi-national and cross-functional[2] teams. He also introduced a western-style pay system.[3] This[4] replaced the seniority pay system that had been deeply entrenched in Japanese culture~~s~~,[5] showing[6] that he lacked cultural intelligence. However,[7] Ghosn then showed that he was challenging Japanese cultural traditions to globalise Nissan. ~~By c~~Creating a global firm ~~it~~[8] demonstrated Ghosn's ability to embrace cultural differences and include them in his organisational culture.

8 errors

It is argued that leaders with global management skills are in high demand among employers,[1] as they enable the company to secure a competitive edge in the ever-changing[2] global marketplace (Hrehová, Svitačová & Klimková,[3] 2017). Ghosn's way of managing Nissan was different to his predecessor, but his new management style resulted in Nissan reporting record profits. A leader's interpersonal skills play~~s~~[4] a vital role when building trust with ~~there~~their[5] employees ([6]Terrell, ~~t~~2018). Also, it is important that global leaders understand the concept of mindful communication (Steers & ~~o~~Osland,[7] 2019). This links with a leader's[8] ability to empathise with their team, improving the quality of the relationships that are formed (Lange & Rowold, 2019). When a leader listens to and understands their followers, there is more likely to be successful~~l~~[9] stress management within the team. **9 errors**

Total: 30 errors

Paragraph 3

1. Multiple adjectives are separated by a comma.

6. The 'ing' verb suggests a following phrase. It does not make sense as a sentence as it is.

8. For more examples of removing excess text, see the teaching pages on 'Pruning excess words' (from page 185).

Paragraph 4

2. When two words are used as one adjective, hyphenate them. See the teaching pages on 'Hyphens' (from page 162) for many other examples.

3. In APA 6th referencing, 'et al.' was only used for 5 or more authors, so 3 authors could be referenced – with a comma between the authors and the date. However, in the new APA 7th referencing guide, 'et al.' is used for 3 or more authors, so here you could change the in-text citation to Hrehová et al., 2017.

4. For verb agreements, see the teaching pages on 'Agreement of verbs' (from page 108).

5. For tips with this homophone, see the teaching page on 'They're/There/Their' (page 159) in the 'Homophones' section.

9. While 'full' on its own is spelt with two ls, the suffix uses only one.

Reflections

Be honest, as you should see how your score improves with each passage you proofread! Finally, reflect on what you have learnt from this piece.

1st Proofreading

Date: _____   Score: _____ /30

What two main points have I learnt?

1.

2.

2nd Proofreading

Date: _____   Score: _____ /30

How did I improve?

1.

2.

What do I still need to remember?

1.

2.

Please use this page for notes

Proofreading Exercise 3 – Final Version!

Carlos Ghosn

Carlos Ghosn is a global business manager known for cutting costs in order to restore a firm's profitability. His career started with the French tyre firm, Michelin; he was involved with the restructuring of Michelin in North America. This essay will explore Carlos Ghosn's approach to global management, using the pyramid model of leadership.

The pyramid model looks at the leadership capabilities that a manager can develop and implement across cultures (Steers & Osland, 2019). The model is in the form of a pyramid to show that there are certain skills and competencies that need to be built upon. The levels also represent the progression of a leader (Mendenhall et al., 2008). The model consists of five levels, which from bottom to top are: global business knowledge; threshold traits; multicultural competence; global management skills; and system skills (Steers & Osland, 2019).

Carlos Ghosn originally wanted to westernise Nissan. He did this by creating western-style, multi-national and cross-functional teams. He also introduced a western-style pay system. This replaced the seniority pay system that had been deeply entrenched in Japanese culture, showing that he lacked cultural intelligence. However, Ghosn then showed that he was challenging Japanese cultural traditions to globalise Nissan. Creating a global firm demonstrated Ghosn's ability to embrace cultural differences and include them in his organisational culture.

It is argued that leaders with global management skills are in high demand among employers, as they enable the company to secure a competitive edge in the ever-changing global marketplace (Hrehová et al., 2017). Ghosn's way of managing Nissan was different to his predecessor, but his new management style resulted in Nissan reporting record profits. A leader's interpersonal skills play a vital role when building trust with their employees (Terrell, 2018). Also, it is important that global leaders understand the concept of mindful communication (Steers & Osland, 2019). This links with a leader's ability to empathise with their team, improving the quality of the relationships that are formed (Lange & Rowold, 2019). When a leader listens to and understands their followers, there is more likely to be successful stress management within the team.

Adapted and used with the kind permission of the author, as indicated in the acknowledgements.

References as provided by the author

Hrehová, D., Svitačová, E., & Klimková, A. (2017). *Educating for Global Leadership*. The Poprad Economic and Management Forum, 162–170.

Lange, S., & Rowold, J. (2019). *Mindful leadership: Evaluation of a mindfulness-based leader intervention. Gruppe. Interaktion. Organisation. Zeitschrift für Angewandte Organisationspsychologie*, 319–335.

Mendenhall, M. E., Bird, A., Maznevski, M. L., Osland, J., & Oddou, G. R. (2008). *Global Leadership: Research, Practice, and Development*. Routledge.

Steers, R. M., & Osland, J. S. (2019). *Management Across Cultures: Challenges, Strategies, and Skills*. Cambridge University Press.

Terrell, T. (2018). *Leadership Theories*. Capella University.

Proofreading Exercise 4

Proofread the following exercise, correcting it and adding punctuation where necessary. Note that not every sentence contains an error. Then compare your version with the corrected one in the next section.

You may like to use an acetate sheet with a drywipe marker pen or some tracing paper on which to mark your errors, so that you can repeat the proofreading exercises at a later date and see how much you have learnt!

Read the passage aloud, as though presenting it in a large lecture room and needing to ensure the students at the back can hear you!
When you project your voice, you need to take pauses for breath, and it becomes easier to see where you have a full sentence break (full stop) or a mini pause (comma). Try it and see!

A SWOT Analysis

Introduction:

The objective of this report is to outline the strengths and weaknesses of Natura, a booming cosmetics company. As well as the opportunities and threats of a potential future market. Through the data and research I have collected it would appear that France is the most viable country for Natura to expand into, for three reasons; to increase profit, diversify risk, and enhance the workforce. **4 errors**

Strengths:

One of Naturas strengths is Research and Development (R&D) the company has invested in technology and research to enable it to produce a new product every three working days (Insead, 2006). This enables natura to constantly offer its consumers new innovative products a practice which is vital in the growing cosmetics industry. Natura has seen revenues grow from investing in R&D, 63% of the companies' revenue was from newly launched or re-launched products (Insead, 2006). Secondly, Natura are passionate about its brand and products. The company cares for the wellbeing of its customers, which lead to consumer loyalty. Thirdly, Natura has 400,000 sales representatives and the lowest turnover ratio among all direct sales companies (Insead, 2006). Minimising recruitment costs and increasing employee loyalty. **12 errors**

Weaknesses:

Natura has weaknesses which need addressing before any expansion into new markets. Natura uses direct selling as a business model but consumers expect to see premium products in premium outlets. Secondly direct selling does not work in low unemployment economies. This is because people do not have time to dedicate to a sales representative they want an immediate option such as online shopping, online markets and advertising worldwide were growing in 2006 (Grande, 2006). Natura's business model would be extremely difficult to take worldwide and ensure every country was promoting Naturas values. This limits growth opportunities. **7 errors**

Opportunities:

France provides opportunities for Natura, as seen in Appendix 1, one of these is the fact that French consumers' respond positively to products with therapeutic scents and textures. Natura's business model of direct selling would allow the company to emphasise these features. Secondly, France has the highest per capita consumption of cosmetics per annum ($230) compared to Brazil ($60), which means that consumers are willing to spend money on cosmetics especially more premium products. If Nature is successful in France this could lead to further opportunities in the EU.

7 errors

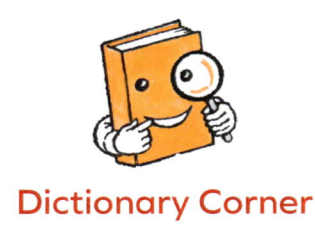

Dictionary Corner

comprise

If you don't know this word, use your dictionary, phone or Google to find the meaning of **comprise** and consider using it in your writing!

Bright ideas to make your writing more academic

Avoid writing in first person unless you are writing a reflective report or have been told to use first person. Sentences can always be turned round to put them into third person.

Thus, instead of writing in Paragraph 1, "Through the data and research I have collected, France is the most viable country for Natura to expand into…", you could write something like: "Data and research have shown that France is the most viable country for Natura to expand into."

See the teaching pages on 'First and third person' for further practice (from page 146).

Note: In APA referencing, appendices (the plural form of 'appendix') are ordered alphabetically – A, B, C and so on. In Harvard referencing, you can use letters or numbers.

Tables and figures are numerically ordered – 1, 2, 3 etc.

Proofreading Exercise 4 – Corrected

Compare your corrected version with the one below. The small raised numbers show where the corrections are: the numbers in pink indicate notes in the margin. Count how many errors you corrected and write your score on the 'Reflections' page overleaf.

Paragraph 1

4 A colon, not a semicolon, introduces a list. See the teaching pages on 'Colons, semicolons, dots and dashes' for further information (from page 128).

Paragraph 2

2 Alternatively, you could use a semicolon if you think the sentence is attached to the first sentence, OR a colon if you believe the second sentence *explains* the first. See the teaching pages on 'Colons, semicolons, dots and dashes' for further information (from page 128).

5 Strictly speaking, this is an example of 'tautology' (using words you don't need) because 'innovative' means 'new'!

7 You could use a full stop here OR a colon to introduce or explain the growth, OR even a dash.

a When a verb is preceded by an adverb ending in 'ly', the two words are NOT joined by a hyphen. See the teaching pages on 'Hyphens' for further information (from page 162).

9 The company is a single entity, so needs a single verb – 'is'.

10 A single subject has 's' on the verb. Check out the teaching pages on 'Agreement of verbs' (from page 108).

12 An 'ing' verb usually indicates an introductory phrase, followed by a full sentence OR a following phrase (that follows a full sentence). This is not a sentence on its own. See the teaching pages on 'Introductory, intermediate and following phrases' (from page 167).

A SWOT Analysis

Introduction:

The objective of this report is to outline the strengths and weaknesses of Natura, a booming cosmetics company,[1] as[2] well as the opportunities and threats of a potential future market. Through the data and research I have collected,[3] it would appear that France is the most viable country for Natura to expand into, for three reasons:[4] to increase profit, diversify risk, and enhance the workforce.

4 errors

Strengths:

One of Natura's[1] strengths is Research and Development (R&D).[2] The[3] company has invested in technology and research to enable it to produce a new product every three working days (Insead, 2006). This enables Natura[4] to constantly offer its consumers new,[5] innovative products,[6] a practice which is vital in the growing cosmetics industry. Natura has seen revenues grow from investing in R&D:[7] 63% of the company's[8] revenue was from newly launched[a] or re-launched products (Insead, 2006). Secondly, Natura is[9] passionate about its brand and products. The company cares for the wellbeing of its customers, which leads[10] to consumer loyalty. Thirdly, Natura has 400,000 sales representatives and the lowest turnover ratio among all direct sales companies (Insead, 2006),[11] minimising[12] recruitment costs and increasing employee loyalty. **12 errors**

40

Weaknesses:

Natura has weaknesses which need addressing before any expansion into new markets. Natura uses direct selling as a business model,[1] but consumers expect to see premium products in premium outlets. Secondly,[2] direct selling does not work in low unemployment economies. This is because people do not have time to dedicate to a sales representative:[3] they want an immediate option,[4] such as online shopping.[5] Online[6] markets and advertising worldwide were growing in 2006 (Grande, 2006). Natura's business model would be extremely difficult to take worldwide and ensure every country was promoting Natura's[7] values. This limits growth opportunities. **7 errors**

Opportunities:

France provides opportunities for Natura, as seen in Appendix ~~1~~ A[1].[2] One[3] of these is the fact that French consumers[4] respond positively to products with therapeutic scents and textures. Natura's business model of direct selling would allow the company to emphasise these features. Secondly, France has the highest per capita consumption of cosmetics per annum ($230) compared to Brazil ($60), which means that consumers are willing to spend money on cosmetics,[5] especially more premium products. If Natura[6] is successful in France,[7] this could lead to further opportunities in the EU. **7 errors**

Paragraph 3

5,6 Here you could use a full stop, a semicolon or a dash, but the capital 'O' is only needed if you choose a full stop.

Paragraph 4

1 In APA 7th referencing, appendices are always ordered alphabetically, whereas in Harvard you can use either numerical or alphabetical ordering.

4 No apostrophe is needed for plurals! See the teaching pages on 'Apostrophes' for further information (from page 119).

6 Try not to lose focus towards the end of a piece. It is easy to overlook a misspelling, because you expect to see the name written correctly!

Reflections

Be honest, as you should see how your score improves with each passage you proofread! Finally, reflect on what you have learnt from this piece.

1st Proofreading

Date: _____   Score: _____ /30

What two main points have I learnt?

1.

2.

2nd Proofreading

Date: _____   Score: _____ /30

How did I improve?

1.

2.

What do I still need to remember?

1.

2.

Please use this page for notes

Proofreading Exercise 4 – Final Version!

A SWOT Analysis

Introduction:

The objective of this report is to outline the strengths and weaknesses of Natura, a booming cosmetics company, as well as the opportunities and threats of a potential future market. Through the data and research I have collected, it would appear that France is the most viable country for Natura to expand into, for three reasons: to increase profit, diversify risk, and enhance the workforce.

Strengths:

One of Natura's strengths is Research and Development (R&D). The company has invested in technology and research to enable it to produce a new product every three working days (Insead, 2006). This enables Natura to constantly offer its consumers innovative products, a practice which is vital in the growing cosmetics industry. Natura has seen revenues grow from investing in R&D: 63% of the company's revenue was from newly launched or re-launched products (Insead, 2006). Secondly, Natura is passionate about its brand and products. The company cares for the wellbeing of its customers, which leads to consumer loyalty. Thirdly, Natura has 400,000 sales representatives and the lowest turnover ratio among all direct sales companies (Insead, 2006), minimising recruitment costs and increasing employee loyalty.

Weaknesses:

Natura has weaknesses which need addressing before any expansion into new markets. Natura uses direct selling as a business model, but consumers expect to see premium products in premium outlets. Secondly, direct selling does not work in low unemployment economies. This is because people do not have time to dedicate to a sales representative: they want an immediate option, such as online shopping. Online markets and advertising worldwide were growing in 2006 (Grande, 2006). Natura's business model would be extremely difficult to take worldwide and ensure every country was promoting Natura's values. This limits growth opportunities.

Opportunities:

France provides opportunities for Natura, as seen in Appendix A. One of these is the fact that French consumers respond positively to products with therapeutic scents and textures. Natura's business model of direct selling would allow the company to emphasise these features. Secondly, France has the highest per capita consumption of cosmetics per annum ($230) compared to Brazil ($60), which means that consumers are willing to spend money on cosmetics, especially more premium products. If Natura is successful in France, this could lead to further opportunities in the EU.

Adapted and used with the kind permission of the author, as indicated in the acknowledgements.

References as provided by the author

Grande, C., 2006. Carat Says Global Advertising Will Grow By 6%. [online] Ft.com. Retrieved from: https://www.ft.com/content/a0060e4a-8855-11db-b485-0000779e2340

INSEAD Business School, 2006. Natura: Expanding Beyond Latin America. CaseCentre, pp.1–24.

Proofreading Exercise 5

Proofread the following exercise, correcting it and adding punctuation where necessary. Note that not every sentence contains an error. Then compare your version with the corrected one in the next section.

> You may like to use an acetate sheet with a drywipe marker pen or some tracing paper on which to mark your errors, so that you can repeat the proofreading exercises at a later date and see how much you have learnt!
>
> There are various homophones in this text – words that sound the same but are spelt differently. How many can you find? See the teaching pages on 'Homophones' (from page 148) for ways to remember how to spell some common homophones.
>
> Look for a passive verb in paragraph 2 and change it to an active one.

Costumes for *The Handmaid's Tale*

In the 1990 film version of *The Handmaid's Tale* the costumes have changed from the book with the handmaids not being as concealed as in the novel where even their faces are hidden by a winged habit one blogger felt that this detracts from the concept of the women being entrapped and hidden in their clothing. "The uniform worn by Natasha Richardson is relatively immodest the hem of the habit ends mid shin revealing precious inches of the Handmaid's legs to hungry, sex starved men while the thin material gives an outline of the womanly shape beneath" (Garbato, 2008) I agree that the costumes where not restrictive enough and were to revealing. Another issue with the films costumes was the way that the wives in blue wore garments that are now very dated as they had fashions of the '90s, with big shoulder pads and '90s hairstyles this ruins the illusion of the piece being set in the future. **14 errors**

The canadian Royal Winnipeg Ballet created an interpretation of *The Handmaids Tale* were the costumes were very angular and minimalistic. "What really works in the ballet are the theatrical values. Liz Vandals wonderful costumes capture Gilead to perfection" (Citron 2013). The angular shapes add to the feel of the theatrical production. I will also be exploring the idea of geometric shapes in my design pushing this idea by adding structure to the garments.

7 errors

All the adaptations of *The Handmaid's Tale* have had a very clear colour pallet often sticking to the original colours in the book. This maybe because of the amount of symbolism within the colours Atwood had chosen. The only characters with dramatic changes seems to be the Jezebels as they are not part of the structure of Gilead, so different costume designers have interrupted these garments differently. **6 errors**

I designed my characters so that they were a large bold presence on stage. This means that their colours needed to reflect their presence. When choosing or dying fabrics, I needed to consider the fact that colour may soften when on stage, so I had to make them more vivid. I kept to the traditional colour palette because it is so regimented, and it shows who the characters are in the dystopian society of *The Handmade's Tale*. **3 errors**

Dictionary Corner

ameliorate

If you don't know this word, use your dictionary, phone or Google to find the meaning of **ameliorate** and consider using it in your writing!

Bright ideas to make your writing more academic

1. Avoid using sentences that begin, "This means that…" or "This is because…". Extend the previous sentence by adding "…, meaning that…", "…, which means…" or "…, because …". Alternatively, you could replace "This means that…" with "Therefore" (followed by a comma to separate it from the main sentence).

2. Go on a treasure hunt for fabulous, descriptive words that lift your writing out of the ordinary! What could you use to replace "pushing this idea" from paragraph 2, line 8? Type in 'enhancing' (without inverted commas), then right click on the word and explore the synonyms presented. There are some great options! Click on your preference to insert it automatically.

Proofreading Exercise 5 – Corrected

Compare your corrected version with the one below. The small raised numbers show where the corrections are: the numbers in pink indicate notes in the margin. Count how many errors you corrected and write your score on the 'Reflections' page overleaf. In this exercise, the insertion of a full stop followed by a capital letter counts as just **ONE error** corrected.

Paragraph 1

1. The comma separates the introductory phrase (setting the scene) from the main sentence. The next two commas separate following phrases, which add more detail. See the teaching pages on 'Introductory, intermediate and following phrases' (from page 167).

5. The quotation has been copied incorrectly, as there needs to be a sentence break here. It could be a full stop, semicolon, a colon or even a dash. I have chosen a colon because the following sentence acts as an explanation as to why the uniform was considered 'immodest'.

7. When two words are joined together to make a single adjective (describing word), join them with a hyphen. See the teaching pages on 'Hyphens' for more information (from page 162).

8. See the teaching pages on 'Th' and 'wh' words (from page 199).

11. See the teaching page on 'To/Too/Two' (page 159) in the 'Homophones' section for help with to, too and two.

a. See the teaching pages on 'Apostrophes' (from page 119) for combining apostrophes with dates.

14. Alternatively, you could join these two sentences with the link word 'which', after a comma instead of a full stop.

Paragraph 2

3. See the teaching page on 'Where/Wear/Were' (page 160) in the 'Homophones' section for the were/where confusion.

6. Avoid the passive tense.

Costumes for *The Handmaid's Tale*

In the 1990 film version of *The Handmaid's Tale*,[1] the costumes have changed from the book,[2] with the handmaids not being as concealed as in the novel,[3] where even their faces are hidden by a winged habit.[4] One blogger felt that this detracts from the concept of the women being entrapped and hidden in their clothing. "The uniform worn by Natasha Richardson is relatively immodest:[5] the hem of the habit ends mid shin,[6] revealing precious inches of the Handmaid's legs to hungry, sex-starved[7] men,[8] while the thin material gives an outline of the womanly shape beneath" (Garbato, 2008).[9] I agree that the costumes were[10] not restrictive enough and were too[11] revealing. Another issue with the film's[12] costumes was the way that the wives in blue wore garments that are now very dated,[13] as they had fashions of the '90s,[a] with big shoulder pads and '90s hairstyles.[14] This ruins the illusion of the piece being set in the future. **14 errors**

The [1]Canadian Royal Winnipeg Ballet created an interpretation of *The Handmaid's*[2] *Tale* where[3] the costumes were very angular and minimalistic. "What really works in the ballet are the theatrical values. Liz Vandal's[4] wonderful costumes capture Gilead to perfection" (Citron,[5] 2013). The angular shapes add to the feel of the theatrical production. I will also ~~be~~ explore[6] the idea of geometric shapes in my design,[7] ~~pushing~~ **developing** this idea by adding structure to the garments. **7 errors**

All the adaptations of *The Handmaid's Tale* have had a very clear colour palet~~te~~**te**[1],[2] often sticking to the original colours in the book. This ~~maybe~~ **may be**[3] because of the amount of symbolism within the colours Atwood had chosen. The only characters with dramatic changes seem~~s~~[4] to be the Jezebels**,**[5] as they are not part of the structure of Gilead, so different costume designers have ~~interrupted~~ **interpreted**[6] these garments differently. **6 errors**

I designed my characters so that they were a large**,**[1] bold presence on stage~~. This~~**, which** means that their colours needed to reflect their presence. When choosing or dy**e**ing[2] fabrics, I needed to consider the fact that colour may soften when on stage, so I had to make them more vivid. I kept to the traditional colour palette because it is so regimented, and it shows who the characters are in the dystopian society of *The Handma~~de~~**id**'s*[3] *Tale*. **3 errors**

Paragraph 3

1. There are 3 variants of this homophone – pallet, palette and palate. See the teaching page on 'Palate/Pallet/Palette' (page 155) in the 'Homophones' section to help you remember which is which.

3. Separate verbs (doing words) – will be/could be/may be. 'Maybe' means 'perhaps'.

4. See the teaching pages on 'Agreement of verbs' (from page 108).

5. See the teaching pages on 'How to use As' (from page 104).

6. The author meant 'interpreted', a word with many of the same letters.

Paragraph 4

1. Separate multiple adjectives (describing words) with a comma. See the teaching pages on 'Commas' (from page 136) for other examples.

2. See the teaching page on 'Dying/Dyeing' (page 152) in the 'Homophones' section for help remembering this homophone.

3. Keep alert for mistakes right to the end of the piece! The spell-checker might not pick up 'handmade', as it is a real word.

Reflections

Be honest, as you should see how your score improves with each passage you proofread! Finally, reflect on what you have learnt from this piece.

1st Proofreading

Date: _____   Score: _____ /30

What two main points have I learnt?

1.

2.

2nd Proofreading

Date: _____   Score: _____ /30

How did I improve?

1.

2.

What do I still need to remember?

1.

2.

Please use this page for notes

Proofreading Exercise 5 – Final Version!

Costumes for *The Handmaid's Tale*

In the 1990 film version of *The Handmaid's Tale*, the costumes have changed from the book, with the handmaids not being as concealed as in the novel, where even their faces are hidden by a winged habit. One blogger felt that this detracts from the concept of the women being entrapped and hidden in their clothing. "The uniform worn by Natasha Richardson is relatively immodest: the hem of the habit ends mid shin, revealing precious inches of the Handmaid's legs to hungry, sex-starved men, while the thin material gives an outline of the womanly shape beneath" (Garbato, 2008). I agree that the costumes were not restrictive enough and were too revealing. Another issue with the film's costumes was the way that the wives in blue wore garments that are now very dated, as they had fashions of the '90s, with big shoulder pads and '90s hairstyles. This ruins the illusion of the piece being set in the future.

The Canadian Royal Winnipeg Ballet created an interpretation of *The Handmaid's Tale* where the costumes were very angular and minimalistic. "What really works in the ballet are the theatrical values. Liz Vandal's wonderful costumes capture Gilead to perfection" (Citron, 2013). The angular shapes add to the feel of the theatrical production. I will also explore the idea of geometric shapes in my design, developing this idea by adding structure to the garments.

All the adaptations of *The Handmaid's Tale* have had a very clear colour palette, often sticking to the original colours in the book. This may be because of the amount of symbolism within the colours Atwood had chosen. The only characters with dramatic changes seem to be the Jezebels, as they are not part of the structure of Gilead, so different costume designers have interpreted these garments differently.

I designed my characters so that they were a large, bold presence on stage, which means that their colours needed to reflect their presence. When choosing or dyeing fabrics, I needed to consider the fact that colour may soften when on stage, so I had to make them more vivid. I kept to the traditional colour palette because it is so regimented, and it shows who the characters are in the dystopian society of *The Handmaid's Tale*.

Adapted and used with the kind permission of the author, as indicated in the acknowledgements.

References as provided by the author

Atwood, M. (1998). *The Handmaid's Tale* (6th ed.). New York: Anchor Books, a division of Penguin Random House LLC.

Citron, P. (2013, October 18). 'Where's the dark heart of RWB's The Handmaid's Tale?'. The Globe and Mail. https://www.theglobeandmail.com › article14914559

Garbato (2008) Reference not given and not subsequently found. Note how critical it is to copy references correctly for easier retrieval later!

Proofreading Exercise 6

Proofread the following exercise, correcting it and adding punctuation where necessary. Note that not every sentence contains an error. Then compare your version with the corrected one in the next section.

You may like to use an acetate sheet with a drywipe marker pen or some tracing paper on which to mark your errors, so that you can repeat the proofreading exercises at a later date and see how much you have learnt!

1. Ensure this is written in 3rd person (no 'I').
2. Look for two words in the 3rd paragraph that need replacing with more appropriate ones.
3. The last paragraph is very long. Where would you put a paragraph break?

Curriculum in the Lifelong Learning Sector

Throughout this assignment I will consider the ideologies and models of curriculum that influence the lifelong learning sector. The school structure implemented in 1839 without a set curriculum. The National Curriculum grew from the 1977 Great Debate, alongside appraisals for teachers and student performance tests. In 1989 the National Curriculum was followed by the introduction of national testing through Ofsted inspections. This is still reflected in schools today, where reform and centralisation is key. In terms of standards, Kelly (2009) suggests, that there is a fall in Literacy and Mathematics standards, which is affected by socioeconomic, diversity and ethics, these include ethnic and social backgrounds of parents. However it is more likely to be reflected in the "inadequacies of an elitist and culturally bias curriculum" (Kelly 2009, p.216). **10 errors**

Gravells et al, (2013, p39) refers to curriculum as a "Big curriculum" and a "Little curriculum". The "Big curriculum" could be classed as an institutions whole curriculum. Whereas the "Little curriculum" may link to the course content. The academic and vocational curriculums are often referred to as separate curriculums (Gravells et al, 2013). Duckworth et al, (2010) described curriculum as a syllabus with set objectives. **7 errors**

Curriculum is embedded within many Ideologies. Scrimshaw (1983) clarified five main ideologies, classical humanism, liberal humanism, progressivism, instrumentalism, and Reconstructionism. To evaluate curriculum four models are used, situational, process, product, and content. Portelli (1987) clarified these as complex and linked the idea that curriculum should be focused on the relationships within the context of curriculum and the underpinning philosophy's. When becoming a teacher it is necessary to formulate and maintain a 'Scheme of Work' (SOW) for every subject in the curriculum. The SOW referenced to in this assignment is for Pearsons BTEC level 2 Health and Social Care course, Unit 12, which is Creative and therapeutic activities in Health and Social Care settings. **13 errors**

Dictionary Corner

assert

If you don't know this word, use your dictionary, phone or Google to find the meaning of **assert** and consider using it in your writing!

Bright ideas to make your writing more academic

1. Buy a small, alphabetised book in which you can write down words you come across that you want to use in future writing. When you are conducting research, look up unfamiliar words in a dictionary and jot those down too, if they could be useful to you. Note down any words you habitually spell incorrectly. Regularly read through the words you have collected to embed them in your memory.

2. Print out a guide to referencing (whether you use APA 7th, Harvard or some other system) and refer to it to check all the punctuation and what is in italics for your in-text citations and references.

Proofreading Exercise 6 – Corrected

Compare your corrected version with the one below. The small raised numbers show where the corrections are: the numbers in pink indicate notes in the margin. Count how many errors you corrected and write your score on the 'Reflections' page overleaf.

In this exercise, the insertion of a full stop followed by a capital letter or replacing a full stop with a comma and removing the capital letter that follows count as just **ONE error** corrected.

Paragraph 1

2 The passive term 'was implemented' is needed here, as a structure could not implement itself!

5 If you read this aloud and take a breath between 'suggests' and 'that', you will hear that it does not sound right to take a breath there, so no comma is needed. A comma is used before 'which' but not before 'that'.

6 'Socioeconomic' is an adjective (a describing word). Here we need a noun (or name) – socioeconomics, like ethics.

7 You need a sentence break here: a full stop or a semicolon would do.

---

1. Removing 'Throughout' and 'I' leaves a very acceptable introductory sentence in 3rd person.

2. In the context of the 3rd paragraph, 'classified' or 'classed' would fit better than 'clarified'. 'Referred to' could replace 'referenced to'.

3. I have suggested where a paragraph break could go to separate the last two paragraphs, instead of having one long paragraph. Do you agree?

Curriculum in the Lifelong Learning Sector

~~Throughout I~~**T**his assignment ~~I~~[1] will consider the ideologies and models of curriculum that influence the lifelong learning sector. The school structure **was**[2] implemented in 1839 without a set curriculum. The National Curriculum grew from the 1977 Great Debate, alongside appraisals for teachers and student performance tests. In 1989**,**[3] the National Curriculum was followed by the introduction of national testing through Ofsted inspections. This is still reflected in schools today, where reform and centralisation ~~is~~ **are**[4] key. In terms of standards, Kelly (2009) suggests~~,~~[5] that there is a fall in Literacy and Mathematics standards, which is affected by socioeconomic**s**[6], diversity and ethics~~,~~**;**[7] these include ethnic and social backgrounds of parents. However**,**[8] it is more likely to be reflected in the "inadequacies of an elitist and culturally bias**ed**[9] curriculum" (Kelly**,**[10] 2009, p.216).

10 errors

Gravells et al~~.~~.[1] (2013, p.[2]39) refer~~s~~[3] to curriculum as a "Big curriculum" and a "Little curriculum". The "Big curriculum" could be classed as an institution's[4] whole curriculum~~.~~, [5]~~W~~whereas the "Little curriculum" may link to the course content. The academic and vocational curriculums are often referred to as separate curriculums (Gravells et al.,[6] 2013). Duckworth et al~~.~~.[7] (2010) described curriculum as a syllabus with set objectives. **7 errors**

Curriculum is embedded within many ~~I~~ideologies[1]. Scrimshaw (1983) ~~clarified~~ **classified**[2] five main ideologies~~,~~:[3] classical humanism, liberal humanism, progressivism, instrumentalism, and ~~R~~reconstructionism[4]. To evaluate curriculum,[5] four models are used~~,~~:[6] situational, process, product, and content. Portelli (1987) ~~clarified~~ **classed**[7] these as complex and linked the idea that curriculum should be focused on the relationships within the context of curriculum and the underpinning philosoph~~y~~ies[8]. **8 errors**

When becoming a teacher,[1] it is necessary to formulate and maintain a 'Scheme of Work' (SOW) for every subject in the curriculum. The SOW ~~referenced~~ **referred**[2] to in this assignment is for Pearson's[3] BTEC level 2 Health and Social Care course, Unit 12, which is '[4]Creative and therapeutic activities in Health and Social Care settings'[5]. **5 errors**

Paragraph 2

1 See the teaching pages on 'Abbreviations' for 'et al' and referencing tips (from page 106).

5 See the teaching pages on 'Th' and 'wh' words (from page 199).

6 The student erroneously referred to two authors in the text as Gravells et al. but the reference clearly indicates just two authors. 'Et al.' is used for three or more authors in APA 7th referencing.

Paragraph 3

1 This is a common noun so does not need a capital letter.

2 Classified?

3 Use a colon to introduce the list of classifications.

7 Classed?

Paragraph 4

1 The 'ing' verb suggests an introductory phrase, separated from the main sentence by a comma. See the teaching pages on 'Introductory, intermediate and following phrases' for further explanation (from page 167).

2 Referred?

Reflections

Be honest, as you should see how your score improves with each passage you proofread! Finally, reflect on what you have learnt from this piece.

1st Proofreading

Date: _____   Score: _____ /30

What two main points have I learnt?

1.

2.

2nd Proofreading

Date: _____   Score: _____ /30

How did I improve?

1.

2.

What do I still need to remember?

1.

2.

Please use this page for notes

Proofreading Exercise 6 – Final Version!

Curriculum in the Lifelong Learning Sector

This assignment will consider the ideologies and models of curriculum that influence the lifelong learning sector. The school structure was implemented in 1839 without a set curriculum. The National Curriculum grew from the 1977 Great Debate, alongside appraisals for teachers and student performance tests. In 1989, the National Curriculum was followed by the introduction of national testing through Ofsted inspections. This is still reflected in schools today, where reform and centralisation are key. In terms of standards, Kelly (2009) suggests that there is a fall in Literacy and Mathematics standards, which is affected by socioeconomics, diversity and ethics; these include ethnic and social backgrounds of parents. However, it is more likely to be reflected in the "inadequacies of an elitist and culturally biased curriculum" (Kelly, 2009, p. 216).

Gravells et al. (2013, p. 39) refer to curriculum as a "Big curriculum" and a "Little curriculum". The "Big curriculum" could be classed as an institution's whole curriculum, whereas the "Little curriculum" may link to the course content. The academic and vocational curriculums are often referred to as separate curriculums (Gravells et al., 2013). Duckworth et al. (2010) described curriculum as a syllabus with set objectives.

Curriculum is embedded within many ideologies. Scrimshaw (1983) classified five main ideologies: classical humanism, liberal humanism, progressivism, instrumentalism, and reconstructionism. To evaluate curriculum, four models are used: situational, process, product, and content. Portelli (1987) classed these as complex and linked the idea that curriculum should be focused on the relationships within the context of curriculum and the underpinning philosophies.

When becoming a teacher, it is necessary to formulate and maintain a 'Scheme of Work' (SOW) for every subject in the curriculum. The SOW referred to in this assignment is for Pearson's BTEC level 2 Health and Social Care course, Unit 12, which is 'Creative and therapeutic activities in Health and Social Care settings'.

Adapted and used with the kind permission of the author, as indicated in the acknowledgements.

References as provided by the author

Duckworth, A. L., Tsukayama, E., & Geier, A. B. (2010). Self-controlled children stay leaner in the transition to adolescence. *Appetite*, *54*(2), 304–308. https://doi.org/10.1016/j.appet.2009.11.016

Gravells, J., & Wallace, S (2013). *The A-Z guide to working in further education.* Northwich: Critical Publishing.

Kelly, A. (2009) *The Curriculum: Theory and Practice.* (Eds, 6). London: Saga Publication.

Pearson Education Ltd, (2016). *BTEC National, Health and Social Care Pearson's qualification Edexcel* Last retrieved from. http://qualifications.pearson.com.

Portelli, J (1987). Perspectives and Imperatives on defining curriculum. *Journal of curriculum and supervision*, 2 (4), 345–367

Scrimshaw, P. (1983). *Purpose and planning in the classroom.* Milton Keynes: Open University Press.

Proofreading Exercise 7

Proofread the following exercise, correcting it and adding punctuation where necessary. Note that not every sentence contains an error. Then compare your version with the corrected one in the next section.

You may like to use an acetate sheet with a drywipe marker pen or some tracing paper on which to mark your errors, so that you can repeat the proofreading exercises at a later date and see how much you have learnt!

1. How many times is the word 'important' used in the exercise below? Right click on the word and select 'Synonyms' to find alternatives. Eight choices are given, but you could also substitute 'crucial' or critical', if more appropriate.

2. Which sentence uses 'also' twice? Remove one of them!

3. In the last sentence of paragraph 1, find a more descriptive word than 'things' to earn a point!

Qualities in a Registered Nurse

As a student training to be a Registered Nurse (RN) it is extremely important that you are trustworthy, reliable, considerate and respectful to everyone, regardless of their age, gender, sexuality, culture, religion or colour, it is also important that you have the skills known as the six Cs communication, courage, commitment, care, compassion, and competence. Most of these are interpersonal skills and are used to deliver the most effective person centred care possible. All these things underpin what is expected of being a professional (NHS, 2012) **6 errors**

As an RN, it is expected that you have the relevant knowledge needed for you to work in your post, that you have completed all mandatory training, and that you only work within your limitations (Health Education England 2011). It is also important that RNs can recognise potential risks, both to the patient, other colleges and themselves, which can be achieved through maintaining there own physical and mental well-being (De Chesnay & Anderson, 2019. **4 errors**

As a student or as an RN you are a roll model to other students, colleagues and the general public. As a professional going into nursing, it is expected that individuals will work to the best of their ability putting each and every patients' best interests and care above all, as person-centred care is the most important goal. It is also important to be aware that you also have a Duty of Candour to all patients and their familys, it is a legal duty that you should always be open and honest. Therefore when there is an incident or mistake during an individuals care or treatment, this should be reported immediately, it is also important that all recordkeeping is a true and accurate account of what is said or done as these documents could be used in a court of law.

10 errors

As an RN, you are also looked at as nursing educators (NEs), because you have achieved a masters nursing degree. Achieving this allows you to teach and help to train upcoming future nurses at collage and university. NEs are still expected to maintain clinical competents even when they are not working on the wards. NEs have a number of roles they play they develop classes and programmes of study, they teach and advice students and oversee clinical practise. They work in teaching hospitals, demonstrating their professionalism, whilst been able to share their strengths, skills, knowledge and experience with the students that are going to become the next generation of nurses. **10 errors**

Dictionary Corner

posit

If you don't know this word, use your dictionary, phone or Google to find the meaning of **posit** and consider using it in your writing!

Bright ideas to make your writing more academic

1. What word begins each paragraph in the text? Try to avoid this kind of repetition in your work. Can you think of other ways of introducing each paragraph?

2. What single word could you use for 'looked at' in paragraph 4?

3. A comma is needed after an introductory word like 'therefore', 'consequently', and 'however' in the same way you use a comma after an introductory phrase. It is not essential to the sentence that follows, so is separated from it by the comma.

See the teaching pages on 'Commas' (from page 136) and 'Introductory, intermediate and following phrases' (page 167) for reinforcement and consolidation of these points.

Proofreading Exercise 7 – Corrected

Compare your corrected version with the one below. The small raised numbers show where the corrections are: the numbers in pink indicate notes in the margin. Count how many errors you corrected and write your score on the 'Reflections' page overleaf.

In this exercise, the insertion of a full stop followed by a capital letter counts as just **ONE error** corrected.

Qualities in a Registered Nurse

Paragraph 1

3. A colon introduces a list.

4. When two words are made into one adjective (describing word), join them with a hyphen. See the teaching pages on 'Hyphens' for more examples (from page 162).

5. Give yourself a mark if you changed 'things' to a more academic word, such as 'values'.

Paragraph 2

3. For tips to help you remember the correct homophone, see the teaching page on 'They're/There/Their' (page 159) in the 'Homophones' section.

Paragraph 3

1. The comma separates the introductory phrase from the main sentence. See the teaching pages on 'Introductory, intermediate and following phrases' for more information (from page 167).

3. Here, the comma separates the main sentence from the following phrase. Again, see the teaching pages on 'Introductory, intermediate and following phrases' for more information (from page 167).

4. See the teaching pages on 'Apostrophes' for how to use the possessive apostrophe (from page 119).

10. (Next page) The comma is needed before the 'as', because you are adding detail to quite a long sentence, so need to pause for breath. See the teaching pages on 'How to use As' (from page 104).

As a student training to be a Registered Nurse (RN),[1] it is extremely important that you are trustworthy, reliable, considerate and respectful to everyone, regardless of their age, gender, sexuality, culture, religion or colour.[2] It is also important that you have the skills known as the six Cs:[3] communication, courage, commitment, care, compassion, and competence. Most of these are interpersonal skills and are used to deliver the most effective person-centred[4] care possible. All these ~~things~~ **values**[5] underpin what is expected of being a professional (NHS, 2012).[6] **6 errors**

As an RN, it is expected that you have the relevant knowledge needed for you to work in your post, that you have completed all mandatory training, and that you only work within your limitations (Health Education England,[1] 2011). It is also important that RNs can recognise potential risks, both to the patient, other ~~colleges~~ **colleagues**[2] and themselves, which can be achieved through maintaining ~~there~~ **their**[3] own physical and mental well-being (De Chesnay & Anderson, 2019).[4] **4 errors**

As a student or as an RN,[1] you are a ~~roll~~ **role**[2] model to other students, colleagues and the general public. As a professional going into nursing, it is expected that individuals will work to the best of their ability,[3] putting each and every patient's[4] best interests and care above all, as person-centred care is the most important goal. It is also important to be aware that you ~~also~~ have a Duty of Candour to all patients and their famil~~y~~**ies**[5]. It[6] is a legal duty that you should always be open and honest. Therefore,[7] when there is an incident or mistake during an individual's[8] care or treatment, this should be reported immediately. It[9] is also important that all recordkeeping is a true and accurate

64

account of what is said or done,[10] as these documents could be used in a court of law. **10 errors**

As an RN, you are also ~~looked at~~ **regarded** as nursing educators (NEs), because you have achieved a master's[1] nursing degree. Achieving this allows you to teach and help to train upcoming future nurses at ~~collage~~**college**[2] and university. NEs are still expected to maintain clinical ~~competents~~**competence**,[3&4] even when they are not working on the wards. NEs have a number of roles they play:[5] they develop classes and programmes of study;[6] they teach and ~~advice~~**advise**[7] students;[8] and oversee clinical ~~practise~~**practice**[9]. They work in teaching hospitals, demonstrating their professionalism, whilst ~~been~~ **being**[10] able to share their strengths, skills, knowledge and experience with the students that[a] are going to become the next generation of nurses. **10 errors**

Total: 30 errors

Paragraph 4

2 For help remembering the difference between 'collage', 'college' and 'colleague', see page 150 in the teaching pages on 'Homophones'.

3 'Competent' is a describing word which (in the English language) cannot be made plural. 'Competence' is the name of a quality, so it is a noun and can have a plural form.

5 A colon introduces the list of roles played, which I would separate with semicolons. See the teaching pages on 'Colons, semicolons, dots and dashes' (from page 128).

7 See the 'Advise/Advice' section on page 148 within the teaching pages on 'Homophones'.

9 This is one of the trickiest homophones! For a good way to remember which is which, see the 'Practice/Practise' section (from page 155) within the teaching pages on 'Homophones'.

10 See the teaching pages on 'Been/Being' (from page 126).

a Strictly speaking, we use 'who' for people, but 'that' can refer to people as well as objects.

Reflections

Be honest, as you should see how your score improves with each passage you proofread! Finally, reflect on what you have learnt from this piece.

1st Proofreading

Date: _____   Score: _____ /30

What two main points have I learnt?

1.

2.

2nd Proofreading

Date: _____   Score: _____ /30

How did I improve?

1.

2.

What do I still need to remember?

1.

2.

Please use this page for notes

Proofreading Exercise 7 – Final Version!

Qualities in a Registered Nurse

As a student training to be a Registered Nurse (RN), it is extremely important that you are trustworthy, reliable, considerate and respectful to everyone, regardless of their age, gender, sexuality, culture, religion or colour. It is also important that you have the skills known as the six Cs: communication, courage, commitment, care, compassion, and competence. Most of these are interpersonal skills and are used to deliver the most effective person-centred care possible. All these values underpin what is expected of being a professional (NHS, 2012).

As an RN, it is expected that you have the relevant knowledge needed for you to work in your post, that you have completed all mandatory training, and that you only work within your limitations (Health Education England, 2011). It is also important that RNs can recognise potential risks, both to the patient, other colleagues and themselves, which can be achieved through maintaining their own physical and mental well-being (De Chesnay & Anderson, 2019).

As a student or as an RN, you are a role model to other students, colleagues and the general public. As a professional going into nursing, it is expected that individuals will work to the best of their ability, putting each and every patient's best interests and care above all, as person-centred care is the most important goal. It is also important to be aware that you have a Duty of Candour to all patients and their families. It is a legal duty that you should always be open and honest. Therefore, when there is an incident or mistake during an individual's care or treatment, this should be reported immediately. It is also important that all recordkeeping is a true and accurate account of what is said or done, as these documents could be used in a court of law.

As an RN, you are also regarded as nursing educators (NEs), because you have achieved a master's nursing degree. Achieving this allows you to teach and help to train upcoming future nurses at college and university. NEs are still expected to maintain clinical competence, even when they are not working on the wards. NEs have a number of roles they play: they develop classes and programmes of study; they teach and advise students; and oversee clinical practice. They work in teaching hospitals, demonstrating their professionalism, whilst being able to share their strengths, skills, knowledge and experience with the students that are going to become the next generation of nurses.

Adapted and used with the kind permission of the author, as indicated in the acknowledgements.

References as provided by the author

De Chesnay, M. & Anderson, B. (2019). *Caring for the Vulnerable: Perspectives in Nursing Theory, Practice, and Research.* Jones & Bartlett Learning.

Health Education England. (2011). *Raising the Bar Shape of Caring: A Review of the Future Education and Training of Registered Nurses and Care Assistants.* https://www.hee.nhs.uk/

National Health Service. (2012). *Compassion in Practice.* https://www.england.nhs.uk

Proofreading Exercise 8

Proofread the following exercise, correcting it and adding punctuation where necessary. Note that not every sentence contains an error. Then compare your version with the corrected one in the next section.

> You may like to use an acetate sheet with a drywipe marker pen or some tracing paper on which to mark your errors, so that you can repeat the proofreading exercises at a later date and see how much you have learnt!
>
> 1. Look out for apostrophes needed. Be aware that some of the punctuation may be incorrect.
> 2. The name of a brand does not need to be in inverted commas or italics. Capital letters are enough.
> 3. Intermediate phrases have commas around them. Look out for these, especially in paragraph 4.
>
> If you are not sure how to use apostrophes (page 119) or want to revise the use of commas (page 136), check out the relevant teaching pages.

The History Behind a Fashion Label

Arthur the Label is a consumer led, luxury collection for women inspired by the miners strike in Yorkshire. The collection entitled '1984' prioritises sustainability and explores the importance of women during the miners strike **5 errors**

The history of the miners' strike is often told from the perspective of men, nonetheless the women of the coalfields played a vigorous part in the making of history. Whether they went out to work, stood on the picket lines made up food parcels, or gave their support to the miners'. This collection highlights the importance of these women during the strike. **7 errors**

Arthur the Label aims to educate customers, by highlighting our impact on the planet and the affects fast fashion have. It eliminates the throw away element of fast fashion replacing it with timeless collections that will be adaptable to each individual and their own divers style. **5 errors**

This collection is an extensive range of products for the modern, energetic woman passionate about sustainability and making less of an impact on our planet. Advanced patternmaking methods are used alongside various construction techniques to ensure all garments are made to a high quality, allowing garments to last a lifetime. Garments are adaptable allowing them to be worn through winter into summer, which allows our consumers to create adaptable outfits. All the garments are made using thoughtfully selected fabrics which are either sourced deadstock fabric, fabrics from existing garments, eco-friendly fabrics or locally sourced fabrics. **5 errors**

This sustainable capsule collection is a approach to give more value to a garment, whilst building relationships with our customers and providing usefull and proactive information about our ever changing climate status. The brand is curated around transparency, so the brands first priority is to be transparent with the consumer. Arthur the Label has gone to the next level to educate their customer on every step of the journey there garments have taken. Including being able to see where in the world each garment has been made. Arthur the Label creates a luxurious way of shopping online, creating an inclusive environment for like minded customers.

8 errors

Dictionary Corner

discrepancies

If you don't know this word, use your dictionary, phone or Google to find the meaning of **discrepancies** and consider using it in your writing!

Bright ideas to make your writing more academic

Try to avoid repeating the same word and phrase.

Count how many times the words 'garment' or 'garments' are used in paragraphs 4 and 5. Tip: Use Control and F (find) and then type in the word 'garment'. All the examples of 'garment' in the text will then be highlighted. Right click on one of the 'garments' and select 'Synonyms'. This will give you a range of options and you can insert one by clicking on the word of your choice. Thus, you could re-write paragraph 5 like this:

Advanced patternmaking methods are used to ensure all garments are made to a high quality, allowing them to last a lifetime. Outfits are adaptable, allowing them to be worn through winter into summer, which allows our consumer to create adaptable ensembles. All the clothes are made using thoughtfully selected fabrics.

Repeat this activity with the words 'allow' and 'fabric' to improve the academic quality of this text.

Proofreading Exercise 8 – Corrected

Compare your corrected version with the one below. The small raised numbers show where the corrections are: the numbers in pink indicate notes in the margin. Count how many errors you corrected and write your score on the 'Reflections' page overleaf.

The History Behind a Fashion Label

Paragraph 1

3 See the teaching pages on 'Apostrophes' for help with this (from page 119).

Paragraph 2

5 'Wh' words like 'which', 'whereas', 'while' and 'whether' often LINK sentences rather than begin them, whereas 'th' words like 'therefore', 'thus', 'this is…' and 'there are…' tend to begin sentences. See the teaching pages on 'Th' and 'wh' words (from page 199).

7 Apostrophes are not needed for plural nouns, unless something belongs to them, like the miners' strike.

Paragraph 3

2 The (singular) subject 'fast fashion' here needs the singular form of the verb. If you turned the phrase around, you would say 'Fast fashion has effects.' See page 148 for help with the 'Affect/effect' homophone and the teaching pages on the 'Agreement of verbs' (from page 108).

5 'Divers' means 'many', whereas 'diverse' means 'different' or 'various'.

Paragraph 4

1 Here, the comma could indicate the missing words 'who is'.

2&3 In this long sentence, using commas to 'bracket' an intermediate phrase makes it easier to read and offers a contrast of tone.

Arthur the Label is a consumer-[1] led, luxury collection for women,[2] inspired by the miners'[3] strike in Yorkshire. The collection entitled '1984' prioritises sustainability and explores the importance of women during the miners'[4] strike.[5] **5 errors**

The history of the miners' strike is often told from the perspective of men.[1] [2]Nonetheless,[3] the women of the coalfields played a vigorous part in the making of history.[4] [5]Whether they went out to work, stood on the picket lines,[6] made up food parcels, or gave their support to the miners.[7] This collection highlights the importance of these women during the strike. **7 errors**

Arthur the Label aims to educate customers, by highlighting our impact on the planet and the effects[1] fast fashion has[2]. It eliminates the throw-away[3] element of fast fashion,[4] replacing it with timeless collections that will be adaptable to each individual and their own diverse[5] style. **5 errors**

This collection is an extensive range of products for the modern, energetic woman,[1] passionate about sustainability and making less of an impact on our planet. Advanced patternmaking methods are used,[2] alongside various construction techniques,[3] to ensure all garments are made to a high quality, allowing garments to last a lifetime. Garments are adaptable,[4] allowing them to be worn through winter into summer, which allows our consumers to create adaptable outfits. All the garments are made using thoughtfully selected fabrics,[5] which are either sourced deadstock fabric, fabrics from existing garments, eco-friendly fabrics or locally sourced fabrics. **5 errors**

This sustainable capsule collection is a**n**¹ approach to give more value to a garment, whilst building relationships with our customers and providing useful**l**² and proactive information about our ever-changing³ climate status. The brand is curated around transparency, so the brand**'s**⁴ first priority is to be transparent with the consumer. Arthur the Label has gone to the next level to educate their customer on every step of the journey ~~there~~**their**⁵ garments have taken**.**,⁶ ~~I~~**i**ncluding⁷ being able to see where in the world each garment has been made. Arthur the Label creates a luxurious way of shopping online, creating an inclusive environment for like-minded⁸ customers. **8 errors**

Total: 30 errors

> **Paragraph 5**
>
> 1 See the 'A/An' teaching pages for an explanation of when to use 'an' (from page 102).
>
> 2 'Full' on its own needs two ls. When it is a suffix, only one l is needed.

Reflections

Be honest, as you should see how your score improves with each passage you proofread! Finally, reflect on what you have learnt from this piece.

1st Proofreading

Date: _____   Score: _____ /30

What two main points have I learnt?

1.

2.

2nd Proofreading

Date: _____   Score: _____ /30

How did I improve?

1.

2.

What do I still need to remember?

1.

2.

Please use this page for notes

Proofreading Exercise 8 – Final Version!

The History Behind a Fashion Label

Arthur the Label is a consumer-led, luxury collection for women, inspired by the miners' strike in Yorkshire. The collection entitled '1984' prioritises sustainability and explores the importance of women during the miners' strike.

The history of the miners' strike is often told from the perspective of men. Nonetheless, the women of the coalfields played a vigorous part in the making of history, whether they went out to work, stood on the picket lines, made up food parcels, or gave their support to the miners. This collection highlights the importance of these women during the strike.

Arthur the Label aims to educate customers, by highlighting our impact on the planet and the effects fast fashion has. It eliminates the throw-away element of fast fashion, replacing it with timeless collections that will be adaptable to each individual and their own diverse style.

This collection is an extensive range of products for the modern, energetic woman, passionate about sustainability and making less of an impact on our planet. Advanced patternmaking methods are used, alongside various construction techniques, to ensure all garments are made to a high quality, allowing garments to last a lifetime. Garments are adaptable, allowing them to be worn through winter into summer, which allows our consumers to create adaptable outfits. All the garments are made using thoughtfully selected fabrics, which are either sourced deadstock fabric, fabrics from existing garments, eco-friendly fabrics or locally sourced fabrics.

This sustainable capsule collection is an approach to give more value to a garment, whilst building relationships with our customers and providing useful and proactive information about our ever-changing climate status. The brand is curated around transparency, so the brand's first priority is to be transparent with the consumer. Arthur the Label has gone to the next level to educate their customer on every step of the journey their garments have taken, including being able to see where in the world each garment has been made. Arthur the Label creates a luxurious way of shopping online, creating an inclusive environment for like-minded customers.

Adapted and used with the kind permission of the author, as indicated in the acknowledgements.

Proofreading Exercise 9

Proofread the following exercise, correcting it and adding punctuation where necessary. Note that not every sentence contains an error. Then compare your version with the corrected one in the next section.

> You may like to use an acetate sheet with a drywipe marker pen or some tracing paper on which to mark your errors, so that you can repeat the proofreading exercises at a later date and see how much you have learnt!
>
> 1. For your 1st point, replace 2 words in line 1 with 1 word to give a more specific verb.
>
> 2. Look out for sentences beginning 'By…'. They use unnecessary words. Can you remove them? See the teaching pages on 'Pruning Excess Words' for help (from page 185).
>
> 3. Where else does an opening sentence use excess or unnecessary words? In paragraph 3, can you also remove double verbs, nouns and adjectives? (Again, see the teaching pages on 'Pruning Excess Words' for help, from page 185.)
>
> 4. Conversely, some words have been omitted and you will need to add them so that the sentences make sense!

Caring for Patients with Dementia

When looking at a patient with dementia it is also important to remember the caregiver and insure that they are fully aware of the condition and its progression, so they know and have some understanding of what to expect. By the caregiver being fully informed this can help them to build a better trusting relationship between themselves and the patient. It is also important to bear in mind the interaction patients have with their caregivers as it is equally important that the caregiver takes care of themselves whilst caring for the patient. **6 errors**

Caregivers are seen as the primary carers of patients suffering with dementia as more often than not they are involved in their day to day living and personal needs and even their daily activities all this can have a psychological impact on the caregiver due to the time and energy that they devote to the patient. **4 errors**

Within the literature it also states that the caregiver are at considerable risk of distress if working with individuals with challenging behavioural issues, and they don't have or use effective coping strategies when feeling stressed and frustrated, when they see the patent shows signs of declining health. This is where non-pharmacological interventions are thought to be the most effective method of improving the, understanding and skills the caregiver and of developing better communication and knowledge, this can lead to a more safer and supportive environment for all involved. **9 errors**

This study found that using multiple approaches the evidence shows that non-pharmacological interventions proved to be more successful in reducing poor patient behaviour with significant benefits to patient's health and well-being whilst it is also important to understand that medication is vital, but need to be aware of the possible side affects, while pharmacological interventions can increase agitation and also have a negative impact in patients' behaviour. **8 errors**

By following these recommendations it will help to break down social stigma around dementia and peoples missunderstanding of it, so they may start to be more understanding when they see challenging behaviour. **3 errors**

Dictionary Corner

penultimate

If you don't know this word, use your dictionary, phone or Google to find the meaning of **penultimate** and consider using it in your writing!

Why is this an appropriate word for this chapter?

Bright ideas to make your writing more academic

Use Control + F (for Find) to see how many times the word 'important' is used in this exercise! Now right click on one of the examples and use the synonyms feature to insert some alternative words.

While long sentences are often fine if they are well punctuated with commas for breaths, paragraph 4 is one long sentence of 67 words! The paragraph could be divided into two sentences, which would make it much easier to read and understand. We will consider this at the end of the next section.

Proofreading Exercise 9 – Corrected and an Additional Pruning Exercise

In this exercise, the insertion of a full stop followed by a capital letter counts as just **ONE error** corrected. A double hyphen also counts as **ONE error**. In paragraph 3, brackets suggest where extra verbs, nouns and adjectives could be removed.

Caring for Patients with Dementia

When ~~looking at~~ **treating**[1] a patient with dementia**,**[2] it is also important to remember the caregiver and ~~i~~**e**nsure[3] that they are fully aware of the condition and its progression, so they know and have some understanding of what to expect. ~~By t~~**T**he caregiver being fully informed[4] ~~this~~ can help them to build a better**,**[5] trusting relationship between themselves and the patient. It is also important to bear in mind the interaction patients have with their caregivers**,**[6] as it is equally important that the caregiver takes care of themselves whilst caring for the patient. **6 errors**

Caregivers are seen as the primary carers of patients suffering with dementia as**,**[1] more often than not**,**[2] they are involved in their day**-**to**-**day[3] living and personal needs and even their daily activities**.**[4] ~~a~~**A**ll this can have a psychological impact on the caregiver[a] due to the time and energy that they devote to the patient. **4 errors**

Within the literature**,**[1] it also states that the caregiver ~~are~~ **is**[2] at considerable risk of distress if working with individuals with challenging behavioural issues, and they ~~don't~~**do not**[3] (have or) use effective coping strategies when feeling stressed (and frustrated), when they see the ~~patent~~ **patient**[4] shows signs of declining health. This is where non-pharmacological interventions are thought to be the most effective method of improving the~~,~~[5] (understanding and) skills **of**[6] the caregiver**,**[7] and of developing better (communication and) knowledge~~,~~**.**[8] ~~t~~**T**his can lead to a more ~~more~~ safe~~r~~[9] and supportive environment for all involved. **9 errors**

Paragraph 1

1. There are other alternatives to 'treating' in the context, like 'reviewing' or 'considering'. Look at the synonyms and choose one you prefer.

5. Separate two adjectives (describing words) with a comma.

Paragraph 2

2. This is an intermediate phrase, which can be lifted out of the sentence without affecting the sense of the sentence. It should, therefore, have commas around it to separate it from the main sentence. See the teaching pages on 'Introductory, intermediate and following phrases' for more examples (from page 167).

a. You could have put a comma here to separate the sentence from the following reason, but the sentence is short enough for the reader not to need to take a breath. However, give yourself a bonus point if you inserted a comma!

Paragraph 3

2. See the teaching pages on 'Agreement of verbs' for further examples (from page 108).

4. 'Patent' is a real word, so the spellchecker would not spot this misspelling of 'patient'!

7. The grammar-checker would say that no comma is needed between these clauses, but the sentence is so long that a pause for breath is needed. The comma also separates the two actions of the interventions.

9. 'More safer' is an example of tautology – using unnecessary words. You talk about being 'more safe' or 'safer', but NOT 'more safer'.

This study found that,[1] using multiple approaches,[2] the evidence shows that non-pharmacological interventions proved to be more successful in reducing poor patient behaviour,[3] with significant benefits to patient's'[4] health and well-being,[5] whilst it is also important to understand that medication is vital, but **prescribers**[6] need to be aware of the possible side ~~e~~effects[7], while pharmacological interventions can increase agitation and also have a negative impact ~~in~~on[8] patients' behaviour. **8 errors**

Following these recommendations will help[1] to break down social stigma around dementia and people's[2] missunderstanding[3] of it, so they may start to be more understanding when they see challenging behaviour. **3 errors**

Total: 30 errors

Paragraph 4

6   Any appropriate subject could be inserted here, although 'prescribers' is suitable in the context.

8   You have an impact ON something, not in it.

Paragraph 5

1   This is perhaps better understood as an improvement rather than a correction. If the original wording is retained, a comma should be added after 'recommendations'.

2   See the teaching pages on 'Apostrophes' for further explanation and practice (from page 119).

Pruning

The penultimate (last but one) paragraph can be pruned from 68 words down to 44! Let's read it through again.

This study found that, using multiple approaches, the evidence shows that non-pharmacological interventions proved to be more successful in reducing poor patient behaviour, with significant benefits to patients' health and well-being, whilst it is also important to understand that medication is vital but (prescribers?) need to be aware of the possible side effects, while pharmacological interventions can increase agitation and also have a negative impact on their behaviour.

Currently, it is one long sentence covering eight lines. If we look for a convenient sentence break, there is an ideal place halfway through, towards the end of line 4. The first sentence can end after 'well-being'. Below are two ways of pruning the first sentence:

1a. Using multiple approaches, the evidence shows that non-pharmacological interventions are more successful in reducing poor patient behaviour, with significant benefits to patients' health and well-being. (25)

1b. This study found that non-pharmacological interventions are more successful in reducing poor patient behaviour, with significant benefits to patients' health and well-being. (22)

'Whilst' is a link word between two sentences, but we have now separated them. As we cannot use 'whilst' to begin the second sentence, 'however' could be more appropriate. Consider these two options:

2a. However, it is important to understand that, whilst medication is vital, there are possible side effects: pharmacological interventions can increase agitation and have a negative impact on behaviour. (28)

2b. However, whilst medication is vital, there are possible side effects: pharmacological interventions can increase agitation and have a negative impact on behaviour. (22)

The best combination to reduce the word count is 1b+2b: 22+22=44, pruning the paragraph by 24 words! You could also remove 'However' if you felt the text still made sense and flowed!

> See the teaching pages on 'Pruning Excess Words' (from page 185) for more practice!

Reflections

Be honest, as you should see how your score improves with each passage you proofread! Finally, reflect on what you have learnt from this piece.

1st Proofreading

Date: _____   Score: _____ /30

What two main points have I learnt?

1.

2.

2nd Proofreading

Date: _____   Score: _____ /30

How did I improve?

1.

2.

What do I still need to remember?

1.

2.

Please use this page for notes

Proofreading Exercise 9 – Final Version!

Caring for Patients with Dementia

When treating a patient with dementia, it is also important to remember the caregiver and ensure that they are fully aware of the condition and its progression, so they know and have some understanding of what to expect. The caregiver being fully informed can help them to build a better, trusting relationship between themselves and the patient.* It is also important to bear in mind the interaction patients have with their caregivers, as it is equally important that the caregiver takes care of themselves whilst caring for the patient.

Caregivers are seen as the primary carers of patients suffering with dementia as, more often than not, they are involved in their day-to-day living and personal needs and even their daily activities. All this can have a psychological impact on the caregiver due to the time and energy that they devote to the patient.

The literature also states that the caregiver is at considerable risk of distress if working with individuals with challenging behavioural issues, and they do not use effective coping strategies when feeling stressed, when they see the patient shows signs of declining health. This is where non-pharmacological interventions are thought to be the most effective method of improving the skills of the caregiver, and of developing better knowledge. This can lead to a more safe and supportive environment for all involved.

This study found that non-pharmacological interventions are more successful in reducing poor patient behaviour, with significant benefits to patients' health and well-being. However, whilst medication is vital, there are possible side effects: pharmacological interventions can increase agitation and have a negative impact on behaviour.

Following these recommendations will help to break down social stigma around dementia and people's misunderstanding of it, so they may start to be more understanding when they see challenging behaviour.

Adapted and used with the kind permission of the author, as indicated in the acknowledgements.

*The sentence could be further improved by rephrasing it, thus:

Being fully informed can help the caregiver to build a better, trusting relationship between themselves and the patient.

> **See the teaching pages on 'Pruning Excess words' (from page 185) for more practice!**

Proofreading Exercise 10

Proofread the following exercise, correcting it and adding punctuation where necessary. Note that not every sentence contains an error. Then compare your version with the corrected one in the next section. This exercise needs pruning too!

You may like to use an acetate sheet with a drywipe marker pen or some tracing paper on which to mark your errors, so that you can repeat the proofreading exercises at a later date and see how much you have learnt!

Watch out for the organisations in this writing. As a single entity, they should be followed by a singular verb, not a plural one!

Highlight the three organisations in the 1st paragraph before you start. The 3rd is not as obvious as the other two but is a public body.

Let's begin by proofreading the passage for errors. Then, on a separate page, we can condense the text.

Midwives and Community Hubs

The NHS are working with the universities to expand the number of midwifery applicants – to help with future increases in the staffing levels. Which could have the potential to help with the community hubs, however it can take up to three years to start to see and feel the effect of this (NHS, 2019). The Royal College of Midwives (2018) have stated that the plan is good and has lots of ambition for the services provided. However, it also analysis what needs to be done to achieve and implement these ambitions. Additionally, the college did welcome last years increase in midwifery numbers implemented by the government (Walton, 2019). **8 errors**

Whilst supporting woman to stop smoking during pregnancy and postnatally a midwife has the potential to change more than one individuals health for the future. Throughout the assignment it has explored the risks of smoking, and the impact it could potentially have on a mother and her baby. The aim of the government is to become a smoke free society within the next five years, with plans for the midwifes to have more input to this through community hubs. This means that as a midwife it is important to support women throughout this change in their pregnancy. This is through working with other agencys and with the women and their families. **9 errors**

Behaviour change theorys have also suggested that the midwife should empower and encourage the women to continue with the changes even after birth. It is important to tackle smoking during pregnancy as children born into a family or an environment of smokers are more likely to smoke in the future. By providing early intervention during pregnancy a midwife can help change the UK figures on smokers in the future. A main area of concern that has been identified during the assignment is the challenge of the amount of time midwives have. The government are putting pressure on the midwives to help support the women and have created community hubs however midwives feel they don't have the time to support the women with the number of staff they have. Behaviour changes take a while to come into affect therefore it is important for midwives to have the time to work consistently with their mums-to-be and allow for the change to happen. **13 errors**

Dictionary Corner

repudiate

If you don't know this word, use your dictionary, phone or Google to find the meaning of **repudiate** and consider using it in your writing!

Bright ideas to make your writing more academic

1. Try not to use 'the' too much. It is used over 40 times in this extract! Sometimes it is not necessary. It is the definite article, so is used for a particular item, as in "The child fell over the dog." When you are talking about plural nouns in general, you do not need 'the'. Thus, in the first sentence you could remove 'the' in two places:

   The NHS (is) working with ~~the~~ universities to expand the number of midwifery applicants to help with future increases in ~~the~~ staffing levels.'

   (See the teaching pages on the definite article for further explanation, page 101.)

2. Compile a list of introductory words and phrases, so you have plenty of choice. The Manchester University Academic Phrasebank offers a wealth of phrases to use in all sections of academic writing:

   http://www.phrasebank.manchester.ac.uk/

Proofreading Exercise 10 – Corrected

Compare your corrected version with the one below. The small raised numbers show where the corrections are: the numbers in pink indicate notes in the margin. Count how many errors you corrected and write your score on the 'Reflections' page overleaf.

Paragraph 1

1. Although the NHS comprises many departments and individuals, it is a single entity, so it needs a singular verb. See the teaching pages on 'Agreement of verbs' (from page 108).

2. 'Which' is a link word (unless it is asking a question), so it should not begin the sentence here. Either change the full stop to a comma or change 'which' to 'This' and begin a new sentence. See the teaching pages on 'Th' and 'wh' words (from page 199).

6. The Royal College is a single subject, so it needs a singular verb.

8. A possessive apostrophe is needed because the increase 'belongs' to the year. For practice doing this, see the teaching pages on 'Apostrophes' (from page 119).

Paragraph 2

6. The plural of midwife is midwives. See the 'Plurals' teaching pages (from page 182).

9. Remember the rule: Change the y to an i when you add an ending. See the 'Plurals' teaching pages for more examples (from page 182).

Midwives and Community Hubs

The NHS ~~are~~**is**[1] working with the universities to expand the number of midwifery applicants – to help with future increases in the staffing levels. [2]~~Which~~**This** could have the potential to help with the community hubs~~,~~**.**[3] [4]~~h~~**H**owever**,**[5] it can take up to three years to start to see and feel the effect of this (NHS, 2019). The Royal College of Midwives (2018) ~~have~~**has**[6] stated that the plan is good and has lots of ambition for the services provided. However, it also ~~analysis~~**analyses**[7] what needs to be done to achieve and implement these ambitions. Additionally, the college did welcome last year**'**s[8] increase in midwifery numbers implemented by the government (Walton, 2019). **8 errors**

Whilst supporting ~~woman~~**women**[1] to stop smoking during pregnancy and postnatally**,**[2] a midwife has the potential to change more than one individual**'**s[3] health for the future. Throughout the assignment**,**[4] it has explored the risks of smoking, and the impact it could potentially have on a mother and her baby. The aim of the government is to become a smoke**-**free[5] society within the next five years, with plans for the ~~midwifes~~**midwives**[6] to have more input to this through community hubs. This means that**,**[7] as a midwife**,**[8] it is important to support women throughout this change in their pregnancy. This is through working with other ~~agencys~~**agencies**[9] and with the women and their families. **9 errors**

Behaviour change ~~theorys~~**theories**[a][1] have also suggested that the midwife should empower and encourage the women to continue with the changes even after birth. It is important to tackle smoking during pregnancy**,**[2] as children born into a family or an environment of smokers are more likely to smoke in the future. By providing early intervention during pregnancy**,**[3] a midwife can help change the UK figures on smokers in the future. A main area of concern that has been identified during the assignment is the challenge of the amount of time midwives have. The government ~~are~~**is**[4] putting pressure on the midwives to help support the women and ~~have~~**has**[5] created community hubs**.**[6] [7]~~h~~**H**owever**,**[8] midwives feel they ~~don't~~**do not**[9] have the time to support the women with the number of staff they have. Behaviour changes take a while to come into ~~a~~**e**ffect[10]**.**[11] [12]~~t~~**T**herefore**,**[13] it is important for midwives to have the time to work consistently with their mums-to-be and allow for the change to happen. **13 errors**

Total: 30 errors

Paragraph 3

a A new subject suggests a new paragraph. Regular paragraph breaks make the text easier to read and look less daunting than a page of dense text!

4 The government is a single subject, so it needs a single verb.

9 Avoid 'contractions' like this.

10 See the teaching page on 'Affect/Effect' (page 148) in the 'Homophones' section for help with this tricky homophone.

Reflections

Be honest, as you should see how your score improves with each passage you proofread! Finally, reflect on what you have learnt from this piece.

1st Proofreading

Date: _____   Score: _____ /30

What two main points have I learnt?

1.

2.

2nd Proofreading

Date: _____   Score: _____ /30

How did I improve?

1.

2.

What do I still need to remember?

1.

2.

Please use this page for notes

Proofreading Exercise 10 – Corrected and Ready to Prune

Midwives and Community Hubs

The NHS is working with the universities to expand the number of midwifery applicants – to help with future increases in the staffing levels. This could have the potential to help with the community hubs. However, it can take up to three years to start to see and feel the effect of this (NHS, 2019). The Royal College of Midwives (2018) has stated that the plan is good and has lots of ambition for the services provided. However, it also analyses what needs to be done to achieve and implement these ambitions. Additionally, the college did welcome last year's increase in midwifery numbers implemented by the government (Walton, 2019).

Whilst supporting women to stop smoking during pregnancy and postnatally, a midwife has the potential to change more than one individual's health for the future. Throughout the assignment, it has explored the risks of smoking, and the impact it could potentially have on a mother and her baby. The aim of the government is to become a smoke-free society within the next five years, with plans for the midwives to have more input to this through community hubs. This means that, as a midwife, it is important to support women throughout this change in their pregnancy. This is through working with other agencies and with the women and their families.

Behaviour change theories have also suggested that the midwife should empower and encourage the women to continue with the changes even after birth. It is important to tackle smoking during pregnancy, as children born into a family or an environment of smokers are more likely to smoke in the future. By providing early intervention during pregnancy, a midwife can help change the UK figures on smokers in the future. A main area of concern that has been identified during the assignment is the challenge of the amount of time midwives have. The government is putting pressure on the midwives to help support the women and has created community hubs. However, midwives feel they do not have the time to support the women with the number of staff they have. Behaviour changes take a while to come into effect. Therefore, it is important for midwives to have the time to work consistently with their mums-to-be to be consistent and allow for the change to happen.

Adapted and used with the kind permission of the author, as indicated in the acknowledgements.

References as provided by the author

National Health Service. (2019). *The NHS Long-term Plan*. Retrieved from https://www.longtermplan.nhs.uk/publication/nhs-long-term-plan/

Royal College of Midwives. (2018). *RCM responds to new maternity package announcement by Department of Health*. Retrieved from https://www.rcm.org.uk/media-releases/2019/january/

Walton, G. (2019). *Strong effective midwifery leadership key to better, safer maternity care*. Retrieved from https://www.rcm.org.uk/news-views/rcm-opinion/2019/

Pruning the work

When you are ready to prune your work, first highlight any words you could remove. Then, think about simplifying phrases and sentences. Are there any double verbs you could reduce to one? Remember there are over 40 uses of 'the'. Are they all needed?

Different editors will reduce a word count in different ways. The version below is not the definitive way, but it gives ideas as to how you can omit words and restructure sentences and phrases to cut out 62 words. Removed words are coloured grey and struck through with a line (~~like this~~), with **added words or letters in green**. An ongoing calculation of the number of words removed is indicated with smaller, light blue lettering, with the running total shown in **bold**.

Proofreading exercise 10 – Pruned!

Paragraph 1

1. Note the double verb, if not triple verb if you count 'to start' as well! One verb will do when you have a strict word count!

Paragraph 2

1. You can choose between 'could have' or 'potentially has'.

Midwives and Community Hubs

The NHS is working with ~~the~~ (1) universities to expand the number of midwifery applicants – to help ~~with future~~ (+2=3) increase~~s in the~~ (+2=5) staffing levels~~.~~, ~~This could have the potential~~ (+5=10) to help with ~~the~~ (+1=11) community hubs. However, it can take up to three years ~~to start~~ (+2=13) to see ~~and feel~~[1] (+2=15) the effect of this (NHS, 2019). The Royal College of Midwives (2018) has stated that the plan is good and ~~has lots of ambition~~ (+4=19) **is ambitious** (-2=17) for the services provided. However, it also analyses what needs to be done to achieve ~~and implement~~ (+2=19) these ambitions. Additionally, the college ~~did~~ (+1=20) welcome**d** last year's increase in midwifery numbers implemented by the government (Walton, 2019).

Whilst supporting women to stop smoking during pregnancy and postnatally, a midwife has the potential to change more than one individual's health for the future. ~~Throughout~~ (+1=21) ~~t~~**T**he assignment~~, it has~~ (+2=23) explored the risks of smoking, and the impact it could ~~potentially~~ (+1=24) have[1] on a mother and her baby. ~~The aim of the government~~ (+5=29) **The government's aim** (-3=26) is to become a smoke-free society within the next five years, with plans for ~~the~~ (+1=27) midwives to have more input ~~to this~~ (+2=29) through community hubs. ~~This means that, as a midwife,~~ (+6=35) **Thus,** (-1=34) it is important ~~to~~ (+1=35) **that midwives** (-2=33) support women through this change in their pregnancy~~.~~, ~~This is~~ (+2=35) through working with other agencies and with ~~the~~ (+1=36) women and their families.

Behaviour change theories ~~have also~~ (+2=38) suggest~~ed~~ that ~~the~~ (+1=39) midwives should ~~empower and~~ (+2=41) encourage[1] ~~the~~ (+1=42) women to continue with the changes even after birth. It is important to tackle smoking during pregnancy, as children born into a family or an environment of smokers are more likely to smoke ~~in the future~~[2] (+3=45) **themselves**. (-1=44) By providing early intervention during pregnancy, a midwife can help change the UK figures on smokers in the future. A ~~main area of~~ (+3=47) concern that **the assignment** (-2=45) has ~~been~~ (+1=46) identified ~~during the assignment~~ (+3=49) is the ~~challenge of the~~ (+3=52) amount of time midwives have. The government is putting pressure on ~~the~~[3] (+1=53) midwives to help support ~~the~~ (+1=54) women and has created community hubs. However, midwives feel they do not have the time to support ~~the~~ (+1=55) women with the number of staff they have. Behaviour changes take a while to come into effect. Therefore, ~~it is important for~~ (+4=59) midwives ~~to~~ (+1=60) **must** (-1=59) have ~~the~~ (+1=60) time to work consistently with their mums-to-be to allow ~~for~~[4] ~~the~~ (+2=62) change(s) to happen.

62 words removed.

Paragraph 3

1 A double verb again. They are lovely words, but when you have to prune your word count one will suffice. You might prefer to keep 'empower' rather than 'encourage'; it's your choice.

2 'In the future' comes at the end of the next sentence as well, so it seems appropriate to omit it here but insert 'themselves' to round the sentence off. It also saves two words!

3 The definite article is not needed here, as the text is referring to women and midwives generally, not a specific group. See the teaching pages on the definite article (from page 101) for more examples.

4 It is unnecessary to say 'allow FOR' in this context. It is colloquial in some dialects but is not academic. 'Allow' gives permission or enables, whereas 'allows for' suggests facilitation.

A more ruthless pruner!

One of my students pruned the first paragraph even more ruthlessly and effectively than I had done. Compare my version with hers!

My version:

The NHS is working with universities to expand the number of midwifery applicants – to help increase staffing to help with community hubs. However, it can take up to three years to see the effect of this (NHS, 2019). The Royal College of Midwives (2018) has stated that the plan is good and is ambitious for the services provided. However, it also analyses what needs to be done to achieve these ambitions. Additionally, the college welcomed last year's increase in midwifery numbers implemented by the government (Walton, 2019). (87 words)

The Ruthless Pruner's Version!

The NHS works with universities to expand the number of midwifery applicants – to increase staffing levels, which could help with community hubs. However, it can take up to three years to feel the effect (NHS, 2019). The Royal College of Midwives (2018) has stated that the plan is good and has analysed how its ambitions can be implemented. Additionally, the college welcomed last year's increase in midwifery numbers implemented by the government (Walton, 2019).

(74 words – a further 13 shaved off my version!)

Notice how efficiently two sentences in the original version, from "The Royal College of Midwives (2018)" to "achieve these ambitions" have been rephrased and condensed, saving 11 words.

Rephrasing goes hand in hand with 'pruning' to reduce a word count. For further examples and exercises, see the teaching pages on 'Rephrasing' from page 191.

TEACHING PAGES

A and the – Indefinite and Definite Articles

A and **An** are indefinite articles – they do not talk about a specific (definite) item.

The is a definite article. When you say, "The dog sat by the table", you are talking about a specific dog at a certain table, not any old dog at any old table!

Some languages, e.g., Estonian, do not have an article before nouns.

In English, we usually use an indefinite article in front of a single noun, but they are not necessary in front of plural nouns, unless we use 'some'.

The definite article is used in front of both singular and plural nouns. Look at the following passage for examples.

Key:

- Single nouns with the indefinite article – a or an
- Plural nouns with either no indefinite article or the use of 'some'
- Single nouns with the definite article – the
- Plural nouns with the definite article – the

I used to pass a greengrocer's shop which had a wooden barrow outside filled with (some) colourful fruit and vegetables. Unfortunately, carved eradicably (!!) on the outside of the barrow were the words apple's, orange's, banana's, carrot's and so on!!!!

Had they been written on in chalk,* I would have rubbed out the apostrophes but, as they were ENGRAVED in, I had to leave them and hope that all the children passing by would not adopt the use of the possessive apostrophe for plurals in their writing for evermore!

Plurals do not require apostrophes!

* As dictionaries explain, when discussing whether chalk is a singular or plural noun, chalk is not countable. You don't say 'a chalk'. What I am really talking about in the passage is 'a piece of chalk', so 'a piece' uses the indefinite article, whereas 'chalk' does not. This is another example of the vagaries of the English language!

The Definite Article – The

If you use 'the' in front of a word like 'book', it suggests a particular book. 'The' is not needed with plural nouns. For example:

> The aim (singular) of the government (a particular one) is to create a smoke-free environment in the UK (singular) with plans (plural) for midwives (plural) to encourage pregnant women (plural) to stop smoking.

✏️ Remove 'the' from plural nouns in the following two sentences:

> The NHS is working with the universities around the country to expand the number of places on the midwifery courses to increase the staffing levels, which could have the potential to help with the community hubs.

> The government is putting pressure on the midwives to help the women to stop smoking in pregnancy.

Correct answers:

> ✓ The NHS (singular) is working with ~~the~~ universities (plural) around the country (singular) to expand the number (singular) of places (plural) on ~~the~~ midwifery courses (plural) to increase ~~the~~ staffing levels (plural), which could have the potential (singular) to help with the* community hubs (plural).

*Here, you could keep 'the', as you are talking about particular community hubs, which are the focus of the essay containing the quote.

> ✓ The government (singular) is putting pressure on midwives (plural) to help women (plural) to stop smoking in pregnancy.

The Indefinite Article – A and An

Many students with whom I have worked have had no idea why 'an' is occasionally used instead of 'a', so don't worry if you don't have a clue either. In fact, it is for reasons of comfort! If you try to say, 'a apple', 'a egg', 'a igloo', 'a orange' or 'a umbrella', it is quite hard on the throat and sounds very guttural. This is because you are trying to pronounce two vowels together. It is much more comfortable to say, 'an apple', 'an egg', 'an igloo', 'an orange' or 'an umbrella'.

Thus, 'an' is used before a noun that begins with a vowel (a, e, i, o & u).

Change the following to the correct 'article':

Actin is specifically folded so it has to stabilise areas with a adenosine nuclide between them.

DNA has an double helix structure to keep it stable.

The scientist had a established formula.

Registered nurses are also looked at as nursing educators, due to the fact that you have achieved an high-level master's nursing degree.

(Note here that if you speak with a dialect that misses out the 'h' at the beginning of 'high', you might put 'an' erroneously.)

Compare your answers with those in the 'Corrected versions' on page 210.

As and Has

> Because of dialects, it can be difficult to hear whether a word begins with an 'h' or not. Hence, we need a rule to help us decide whether the word we need is 'as' or 'has'. So, here it is!

Has

If the word is next to a doing word (a verb), it will **usually** be 'has', making the verb go into the past tense. For example,

The sun has gone down, and the moon has come out.

In recent years, there has been an increase in the core temperature of the earth.

Over the years, alcohol consumption has increased, despite the negative effects associated with alcohol.

My jumper has shrunk in the wash.

➤ **Put 'has' in the correct place in these sentences:**

This disciplinary panel discussed what the student as done to improve his attendance so far.

Most residents agreed that the provision of public transport as improved in recent years.

President Biden as replaced Donald Trump as President of the USA.

As there as been a case of Covid 19 among the restaurant staff, the meal as been cancelled. **(2 to replace)**

✓ Compare your answers with those in the 'Corrected versions' on page 210.

How to Use 'As'

'As' in an introductory phrase:

If 'as' is used at the beginning of a sentence, it is an introductory phrase, followed by a comma:

> **As well as capability,** the woman needs to have the social and physical opportunity.

> **As a midwife,** it is also important that the motivation, empowerment, and encouragement do not stop after the referral has been made.

> **As I did not know the music I was conducting,** I did not know the tempo or dynamics.

'As' in a following phrase:

Often, 'as' is used to link a following phrase that provides a reason or explanation (instead of using 'because'). If it is a following phrase, it follows a comma:

> It takes time and determination to stop smoking, **as** smoking is an addiction.

> ***TIP:***
>
> If you have a long sentence and need to give yourself pauses for breath, look for **'as', because' and 'which'** and put a comma in front of them. Often the sentence could have ended with a full stop just before the word, but you are going on to give more detail or an explanation in a following phrase, which follows a comma.

'As' in an intermediate phrase:

Example 1:

> This means that**, as a midwife,** it is important to support women throughout this change in their pregnancy.

The acid test whether this has been correctly punctuated is to remove the phrase in between the commas. If the sentence reads alright without it, you have punctuated it correctly!

Here, the sentence without the intermediate phrase reads perfectly:

> This means that it is important to support women throughout this change in their pregnancy.

Bingo! Job done!

'As' at the beginning or end of a sentence:

Make it clear whether your 'as' phrase ends the previous sentence or begins the next one!

Read this aloud to decide which sentence the 'as' phrase is attached to. You have a choice.

Example 2:

> An outdoor scarecrow trail allows social distancing to be maintained, as you view the scarecrow from the pavement, you do not need to go into someone's garden.

Either it is punctuated like this:

> An outdoor scarecrow trail allows social distancing to be maintained, as you view the scarecrow from the pavement. **You** do not need to go into someone's garden.

Or like this:

> An outdoor scarecrow trail allows social distancing to be maintained. **As** you view the scarecrow from the pavement, you do not need to go into someone's garden.

Which do you think is correct? There is no definitive answer: the sentence can be punctuated and read either way.

Abbreviations in References

References use several abbreviations, and it is important to use them correctly.

The most common mistake is with **et al**.

Et al is short for the Latin phrase 'et alia', meaning 'and others'. Whenever you abbreviate a word, you put a full stop at the end of the shortened word. Thus, 'al' has a full stop at the end of it:

> According to Jones **et al.** (2015)…

- If you are using **et al.** as part of an in-text citation, you need to separate it from the date with a comma, just as if the in-text citation was **(Smith, 2010)**. So, you write **(Jones et al., 2015)**. It looks very strange having a full stop next to a comma, but it is correct, trust me!
- If you do not know the date of, for example, an online image, you abbreviate 'no date' to **n.d.** – in both the in-text citation and the reference list.
- If you are indicating the page number of a reference, abbreviate 'page' to **p.** for 1 page or **pp.** for more than one page, e.g., p.12 or pp.15–20.
- Use **Ed.** or **Eds.** in brackets after the names of the editors in the reference list:

    Harmon, W. (Ed.). (1992). *The Top 500 Poems*. Columbia.

    > **Note:** to avoid confusion, in APA 7th guidelines the lower case 'e' is used for the abbreviation of 'edition' to **ed.**, as in **2nd ed.**, while Harvard referencing uses **edn**.

Other abbreviations

Note which ones are followed by a full stop **and** a comma!

- **e.g.,** – short for the Latin *exempli gratia* – **'for example'**
  (Always put a comma after it because it will be followed by an example.)
- **etc.** – short for *et cetera*, which in Latin means **'and so on'**
- **i.e.,** – short for *id est* – **'that is to say…'**

The next 3 are not as commonly used:

- **vs.** – **'versus'** However, in legal citations use *v.* in italics instead.
- **cf.** – This is short for the Latin word **'confer'** so we use it in place of **'compare'** (used to compare contrasting information).
- **viz.,** – **'namely'**

The following is an example of an abbreviation that is not used with APA referencing, but may be seen in research papers and academic journals:

- **ibid.** – short for ibidem, used in citations to refer to the previously mentioned source

Excellent examples of each abbreviation can be found in the APA Style Blog at www.apastyle.org.

Agreement of Verbs

A verb is a doing word, and a regular verb is 'conjugated' in the present tense, thus:

I love	I walk
You love	You walk
He/she/it loves	He/she/it walks
We love	We walk
You (plural) love	You (plural) walk
They love	They walk

Question: Which one is different to the rest in each group?

Answer: The third person (he/she/it) differs because it ends in an 's'.

Sometimes it is difficult to hear the 's' at the end of the verb (e.g., 'suggests'), so many people miss it out. This can affect the whole flow or sense of the sentence, so we need to ensure we use the correct agreement. Where is the 's' missing in the sentence below?

Another intervention that would be beneficial is a diet plan, which suggest changes that can be made to Adam's diet, in order to manage his diabetes.

The subject of the following phrase in the red sentence is 'a (single) diet plan', so the verb that follows it should be the single 'suggests'.

Another intervention that would be beneficial is a diet plan, which **suggests** changes that can be made to Adam's diet, in order to manage his diabetes.

Think: Single subject – 's' on the verb.

Question: What is wrong with the statement in red below?

Social work and inter-professional work promotes information-sharing and cohesion to deliver a good standard of service.

There are two subjects to this sentence – **social work and inter-professional work** – so we need the plural verb to go with them. The plural form of a regular verb does not have an 's' at the end, so it must be written 'promote'.

Social work and inter-professional work **promote** information-sharing and cohesion to deliver a good standard of service.

Correct the appropriate verb in these sentences:

The legato notes in the bass makes the listener feel very relaxed.

Writing development plans enable the individual to develop their learning skills.

Membership decline because of the ageing membership profile.

I have gained an understanding of some of the daily responsibilities of a social worker and the issues families experiences.

The main argument addressed in the debate is that adult care needs are often multiple and intersects with other issues.

Compare your answers with those in the 'Corrected versions' on page 210.

Plural Authors

A common error occurs when using 'et al.' if you do not realise that 'et al.' means there is more than one author, as in the example below:

Popay et al. (2006) states that thematic analysis may lack transparency due to when and how the themes have been allocated and identified.

The plural form of 'states' is 'state'. I know this is very strange, because you would think that if you have an 's' on the end of a noun to indicate a plural noun, you would also have an 's' on a plural verb. Unfortunately, it is one of the peculiarities of English grammar that we don't! Thus, the statement above should be rewritten:

Popay et al. (2006) state that thematic analysis may lack transparency due to when and how the themes have been allocated and identified.

✏️ **Change these sentences so that the verb agrees with the subject.**

Peters et al. (2013) claims younger nurses are reported to have a stronger fear of death, possibly because they may not be experienced or well skilled in dealing with the impact on their emotions.

Other researchers that has conducted some cross-cultural research is Bleidorn et al. (2013). **(2 to change)**

✓ Compare your answers with those in the 'Corrected versions' on page 211.

Irregular verbs

Irregular verbs are different again. A good example is the verb **'to be'** in the present and past tense:

Present tense	Past tense
I am	I was
You are	You were
He/she/it is	He/she/it was
We are	We were
You (plural) are	You (plural) were
They are	They were

Question: How is the following sentence in red incorrect?

There was 80 guests at the wedding breakfast.

If you are not sure, turn the statement around so that it says '80 guests was there at the wedding breakfast'. That doesn't sound right, does it? 80 guests are more than one, so we need the <u>plural</u> form of the past tense, 'were', rather than the single form of the past tense, 'was'. Thus, the sentence should read:

There <u>were</u> 80 guests at the wedding breakfast.

Change these sentences so that the verb agrees with the subject.

We must ensure the nitrogen base of the DNA cell are not damaged.

There are now a broader set of child wellbeing outcomes to apply to each case.

I care about others, I have compassion and are always willing to put others' needs before mine.

There is still numerous barriers we could have to face.

The provision of essential information and resources are vital for service users' wellbeing.

Before I were diagnosed with dyslexia, I just thought I wasn't as bright as other students was. **(2 to change)**

Compare your answers with those in the 'Corrected versions' on page 211.

The verb **'to have'** can also cause problems in the present tense, when again the 3rd person singular has a different form – **'has'**.

> I have
>
> You have
>
> He/she/it **has**
>
> We have
>
> You (plural) have
>
> They have

What is wrong here?

Different decisions made during the creative process has a big impact on the viewer's experience.

The 'different decisions' are plural but the verb that is used about the decisions is the singular form 'has'. It needs to say:

Different decisions made during the creative process <u>have</u> a big impact on the viewer's experience.

Correct the verb that is wrong in the following sentences:

The course of antibiotics have been completed.

The competition for leisure time have caused relative market growth to slow.

Wembley Park is increasingly trying to attract visitors into the area through various entertainment and hospitality outlets that has been opened.

The questionnaire results confirm that most residents agree that public transport links has improved since the construction of Wembley Stadium.

The documentary showed what goes into the making of images and how the different decisions that are made during the creative process has a big impact on the viewer's experience.

Other parameters used in the article are: the employment the events held at the stadium has provided, money generated through events and whether the area have retained that money. **(2 to find.)**

✓ Compare your answers with those in the 'Corrected versions' on page 211.

The verb **'to do'** is another irregular verb:

In the present tense, all except the third person singular use **'do'**. In academic assignments we are usually required to write in the third person, so we write he/she/it **'does'**. The past tense causes us no problems, as every person uses **'did'**.

> *TIP:*
>
> Watch out for organisations or groups of people that act as a single entity. For example, although we know a football team has 11 players, the verb to accompany a team is usually single, so we say:
>
> The team <u>is</u> wearing its new strip today.
>
> If you don't like how that sounds, you can always rephrase it thus:
>
> The team's players are wearing their new strip today.

✏️ **Correct the verb in these sentences:**

The government want to reduce maternal and neonatal mortality by 2025.

The World Health Organisation (WHO) have termed Covid 19 a pandemic.

The United Nations (UN) are made up of 193 member states.

The NHS have published a new plan called 'NHS Long Term'.

The Royal College of Midwives (RCM) have approved the plan for community hubs.

The Parish Council have twelve members.

The NHS are working with universities around the country to expand the number of applicants for nursing courses.

The cohort were clearly in peak physical condition.

The Higher Education Statistics Agency (HESA) collect individual university statistics on behalf of the UK government to inform the public of a university's performance.

✓ Compare your answers with those in the 'Corrected versions' on pages 211 and 212.

Challenge 1

✏️ Make the verbs agree in this exercise.

The number of errors is indicated at the end of each paragraph.

A Critical Appraisal Skills Programme (CASP) were used to assess the quality of the individual articles selected. This systematic process incorporates trustworthiness, ensuring relevance, and confirm the results of each individual article (Critical Appraisal Skills Programme, 2018). The allocated studies for the review was cohort studies (n=3) and RCTs (n=2). Two different CASP checklist tools were used, based on the specific design. There is three sections to the CASP tool, which aims to analyse the validity of the articles. A quality score were used, based on these three sections and questions answering Yes, No or Unclear. Those answering No or Unclear were used to assess the reasoning for these answers. A quality assessment table were constructed, based on the CASP forms, which were then rated as either high, medium and low quality. **(6 errors)**

Thematic analysis is the discovery of patterns within content, in which themes are developed and analysed as a whole and brings together data to synthesise. The variable outcomes within the studies is extracted and reported as themes within this literature review, in a similar way that conceptual themes are derived from qualitative data. Experts in the field states that thematic analysis lack transparency, due to when and how the themes are allocated and identified. **(4 errors)**

A Prisma Flow diagram were then constructed as a visual presentation of the search strategy. PRISMA stands for: Preferred Reporting Items for Systematic Reviews and Meta-Analysis and take into consideration a four-phase flow diagram process that ensure transparency. However, it is displayed in a simplistic manner which do not include the detail of how the systematic review or meta-analysis is conducted. **(4 errors)**

✓ Compare your version with the 'Corrected version' on pages 212 and 213.

References as kindly supplied by the student authors in order of appearance

Popay, J., Roberts, H. M., Sowden, A., Petticrew, M., Arai, L., Rodgers, M., & Britten, N. (2006). *Guidance on the conduct of narrative synthesis in sytematic reviews*. Institute for Health Research.

Peters, L., Cant, R., Payne, S., O'Connor, M., McDermott, F., Hood, K., Morphet, J., & Shimoinaba, K. (2013). How death anxiety impacts nurses' caring for patients at the end of life: a review of literature. *The open nursing journal, 7*, 14–21. https://doi.org/10.2174/1874434601307010014

Bleidorn, W., Klimstra, T. A., Denissen, J. J., Rentfrow, P. J., Potter, J., & Gosling, S. D. (2013). Personality maturation around the world: A cross-cultural examination of social-investment theory. *Psychological science, 24*(12), 2530–2540.

Although

> Many people use 'Although' as an introductory word in the same way they might use 'Therefore,' or 'Consequently,' and put a comma after it. However, 'although' is <u>not</u> an introductory word in itself, but it does introduce what is called 'a subordinate clause which contains a statement.'

Here is an example:

> Although a positive message was put forward, there are many other factors behind drinking alcohol.

The main sentence is: **'There are many other factors behind drinking alcohol.'**

The statement that comes before it is subordinate to the sentence: **'a positive message was put forward'.**

This could be a sentence in its own right, but we link it to the main sentence by using 'although'. This now becomes an introductory phrase, separated from the main sentence by a comma.

An 'although phrase' may come at the beginning, in the middle, or at the end of a sentence. If it is in the middle, as in the example in green below, it acts like an intermediate phrase and has commas around the phrase. (See the teaching pages on 'Introductory, intermediate and following phrases', from page 167.)

> I was offered a huge piece of chocolate cake and, although I was supposed to be on a diet, I could not resist it!

If the 'although phrase' is at the end of a sentence, a comma is placed before it, as in this example:

> I love going ice-skating with my friends, although I fall over every time.

▶ Put commas after, around, or before the 'although phrases' below:

> Although it is no longer an offence to take one's own life it remains an offence to assist a suicide.

117

The motives behind drinking alcohol are multifactorial and although alcohol may provide a short-term solution it can contribute to disease and premature death long term.

Although most of the students who visited the health promotion stand agreed that the promotion of alcohol awareness was good they were limited to completing a questionnaire.

Steve Reich is arguably one of the most influential composers of the twentieth century although his own work was influenced by Bartok and other well-known composers.

In 2005, it was found that almost a third of mothers in England smoked in the last 12 months before pregnancy (National Institute for Health and Care Excellence [NICE], 2010) although smoking among women who are pregnant has fallen in recent years.

NICE. (2010). *Smoking: Stopping in pregnancy and after childbirth.* Retrieved from: https://www.nice.org.uk/guidance/ph26/chapter/2-Public-health-need-and-practice

✓ **Compare your answers with those in the 'Corrected versions' on page 213.**

Apostrophes

Many students omit apostrophes because they are unsure where to use them, but they are not alone in their uncertainty. There is confusion generally, regarding how and when to use apostrophes. In fact, there are two types of apostrophe – to show possession or omission. Both will be explained below.

Apostrophes for Possession

The possessive apostrophe is used to show when something belongs to someone, or they 'possess' something, as in the cat's whiskers, the company's plans or the planets' orbits.

Unfortunately, apostrophes are often erroneously added to plural words, where they are NOT needed. To illustrate this, I tell my students the following story.

> I used to pass a greengrocer's shop which had a wooden barrow outside, filled with all sorts of colourful fruit and vegetables. Unfortunately, permanently carved on the outside of the barrow were the words apple's, orange's, banana's, carrot's and so on!!!! Had they been written on in chalk, I would have gone and rubbed out the apostrophes but, as they were ENGRAVED in the wood, I had to leave them and hope that children passing by would not adopt the use of the possessive apostrophe for plurals in their writing for the rest of their lives!

Plurals do not require apostrophes!

The possessive apostrophe shows when something belongs to someone.

If you want to write about a particular university and its logo or VC or degree courses, these all belong to the university, so we write the university's logo or the university's VC or the university's degree courses. Note that the apostrophe goes after the word university, because the university is the possessor.

If you are talking about **lots of students** and their digs, you would write the students' digs. Note that this time the apostrophe goes after the word students, because the possessors are plural students.

If you are not sure where the apostrophe goes, turn the phrase around and say: **the digs of the students**.

In this case, put the apostrophe after the word **students – the students' digs**.

OR, with the singular version, write: **the logo of the university**.

In this case, put the apostrophe after the word **university – the university's logo**.

> Where an apostrophe is needed, there will usually be two nouns (naming words) together and the first one **will end in an 's'**, with an apostrophe before or after the 's' e.g., **Chelsea's car, the athlete's trainers** and **the students' fees**. Sometimes, there are three nouns together, as in **my friend's daughter's house**, so two apostrophes are needed, because the friend has a daughter, and the daughter owns a house.

It is important to make the sense of writing clear, by inserting the apostrophe in the correct place. For example, where do you put the apostrophe in the following sentence?

The parents treatment of the child was a concern to Social Services.

Is it just one parent who is mistreating the child or is it both? The only way we know is by the correct use of the apostrophe. If it is **one parent**, the sentence will be punctuated like this:

The **parent's** treatment of the child was a concern to Social Services.
(The treatment by [just one] parent was a concern…)

But if **both parents** are at fault, it would be punctuated like this:

The **parents'** treatment of the child was a concern to Social Services.
(The treatment by [both] parents was a concern…)

> **TIP: A three-step rule for apostrophes**
>
> 1. Look for the name of the possessor or owner of something.
> 2. Put the apostrophe after the name.
> 3. Add an 's', unless there is already one before the apostrophe.
>
> For example: the tutor's study, the women's changing room, the boss' car and the officers' mess.

Put apostrophes in the correct places in the following:

That dogs lead has broken.

The three dogs owners were shouting at them.

The ginger cats milk had spilt everywhere.

York Colleges principal is retiring.

Not all the actors scripts were delivered to them on time.

The UK governments plan backfired!

The planets orbits are almost circular whereas a comets orbit is elliptical. **(2 to find)**

In the orchestra, all the musicians attention was focused on the conductors baton. **(2 to find)**

If the noun is plural to start with – like sheep, men or women, the apostrophe will come after the noun (the possessor) – not after the 's'.

E.g., The Women's Institute. (The Institute belongs to the women.)

Put apostrophes in the correct places in the following:

The mens team was very successful.

The sheeps trough was full of water.

The childrens playground was colourful and inviting.

Princess Diana was known as "the Peoples Princess".

When a name that does not end in 's' suddenly has an 's' at the end, it indicates possession, so an apostrophe should precede the 's'.

If a name ends in 's', then we can put the apostrophe after the full name, as in Tess' book or Ross' studies. The following sentence models both versions:

I will be using Rolfe's structure rather than Gibbs' reflective cycle.

Sometimes, people put an extra 's' after a name ending in 's', but in Tess's book, 's' is used three times! However, James's car only uses two. Either ending is acceptable. The Newcastle United football stadium is St. James' Park, while one of the royal parks in London is St. James's Park!

Put apostrophes in the correct places in the following sentences:

This finding suggests that frequent intervention could have an impact in increasing participants perceived severity of their condition and subsequent behaviour change. **(1 apostrophe to insert)**

Multi-agency working is vital to effective safeguarding and child protection. The team is formed around each individual service users concerns. **(1 apostrophe to insert)**

The interviews will be analysed to collect data for both focus groups discussions. **(1 apostrophe to insert)**

At the universitys health centre, the podiatrist addressed Joes feets bunions. **(3 to insert)**

The dentists opinion was that Tinas teeths enamel had worn away. **(3 to insert)**

Due to Harrys mothers strong love shielding Harry, Voldemorts spell rebounded on him. **(3 to insert)**

Compare your answers with those in the 'Corrected versions' on pages 213 and 214.

Exception to the rule!

We do not use the possessive apostrophe when something belongs to 'it', e.g., **the dog has buried its bone.** The reason for this is that we use an apostrophe to indicate the missing letter in the contraction 'it's, when we mean 'it is'. This leads us nicely to the second type of apostrophe – to show omission in contractions.

Apostrophes in Contractions

When we contract two words to become one word, usually in conversation, we indicate where letters have been pushed out by inserting an apostrophe. Sometimes, just one letter is pushed out, as when **is not** is contracted to **isn't**. If two letters are omitted, just one apostrophe is used to indicate the omission, as when the single word **cannot*** becomes **can't**.

*It is hard to say 'can not' as two separate words, which is probably why we just say 'cannot' as a single word.

Note that contractions are NOT advised in academic writing.

▶ **Contract the following and insert the apostrophe where appropriate:**

(Note that *had* and *would* are both abbreviated to '*d*. Also, look out for the tricky last example in the list!)

I have	are not	you are	would not
we had	there would	is not	you have
could not	I will	it is	should have
there will	did not	shall not	

▶ **Write these contractions in their full form, without an apostrophe:**

(Again, look out for the tricky last example!)

I'd	she's	wasn't	they'd	we've
shouldn't	it'd	can't	we're	you'd
they'll	would've	there's	don't	won't

✓ Compare your answers with those in the 'Corrected versions' on page 214.

A Note About Letters and Dates:

In American English, an apostrophe is used to indicate plural letters, as in

> Carol got two A's and a B in her A levels.

Presumably, this is because As could be misread as the word 'as'.

Americans might also write about the 1960's or temperatures being in the 30's. However, in English we use the apostrophe to indicate possession or omission and there is nothing belonging to the 1960s, nor is any letter missing. If you were writing about 1960's fashion, you could use the apostrophe, because the fashion belongs to the decade. Similarly, the '60s would feature an apostrophe, because the 19 that should be in front has been omitted.

> Unfortunately, the default spell-checker on most computers and laptops is set to American English, so you may be prompted to use apostrophes for letters and dates, as well as to change the spelling of 'colour' to 'color' and 'realise' to 'realize'. It is worth changing the language of your spell-checker from English (United States) to English (United Kingdom)!

Remember that in English we do not use apostrophes for plurals!

Been/Being

'Been' and 'being' come from the verb 'to be' and it can be quite hard to hear the difference between them. Fortunately, there is a little trick to help us decide which is the right word to use in the context. It refers to a rather derogatory phrase about people who were once famous but are no longer, who are described as '**has beens**'!

'Been' is always attached to the verb 'to have', so if the choice of been/being has a 'h' word in front, like '**has**', '**had**', '**have**' or '**having**', choose 'been'.

Thus,

> The course **has been** a huge success.
>
> When the results came back, I **had been** diagnosed with dyslexia.
>
> An interactive activity could **have been** more effective.
>
> **Having been** a primary school teacher originally, my mum is good with children.

(For the visual learners among you, picture the green 'beens', rather like green beans!)

Conversely, if you look at the following sentences, there is no 'h' word in front of 'being':

> Being able to communicate effectively is essential when dealing with patients.
>
> As a registered nurse, you are required to display the six Cs: communication, courage, commitment, care, compassion and competence. All these skills underpin being a professional.
>
> It is also important to understand that being a professional is linked to learning.

Insert 'been' or 'being' in these sentences:

> I was about to face my toughest challenge yet – an undergraduate degree. It wasn't going to be easy, especially not _____ able to read all that well.
>
> There have _____ some amazing shooting stars in the skies recently.
>
> A fine for not adhering to social distancing rules has _____ introduced.

Having _____ evicted by her landlord, the student had to find new accommodation.

I am _____ very lazy today!

B_____ a professional musician has _____ my ambition since childhood.

Note: In the way many of us speak today, 'could have been' often sounds like 'could of been'. We also say, 'should have been', 'must have been' and 'would have been'. Remember that 'have' goes with 'been' – 'have been'.

In some dialects, 'been' is pronounced as 'bin', as in 'Have you bin shopping?' or 'Where have you bin?' When writing, remember to use 'been', not 'bin'. Notice that the 'have' is still there, even if, in the question "Have you been shopping?", the sentence 'You have been shopping' is turned round and 'have' is separated from 'been' by the pronoun 'you'.

There are one or two corrections needed in each sentence below:

It would of been more effective to have an interactive activity for students to measure what they thought a unit of alcohol was; they could of used water in place of the alcohol.

The footballers should of known better than to go out drinking the night before the match.

I would of thought the government could of cut inflation by now.

The University should of ensured Freshers' Week went ahead with online activities.

Lectures should not of been cancelled. Pre-recorded lectures could of been shown online instead.

The student's marks must not of been added up correctly. She could of failed had her tutor not realised the grade was inaccurate.

Compare your answers with those in the 'Corrected versions' on pages 215 and 216.

Colons and Semicolons, Dots and Dashes

Colons

A colon introduces a list, a quotation or an explanation. For example,

To make Yorkshire puddings, you will need: flour, eggs, milk, and some dripping to cook them in.

The following is a quote by Leonardo da Vinci: "Art is never finished, only abandoned."

My brother is joining an orchestra: he is an excellent saxophonist.

(A colon is used here because the second sentence explains the first, so the colon replaces 'because'.)

No matter what the purpose of the image, they all have one thing in common: they are there to serve a purpose.

(In this last example, you could also use a dash instead of a colon – for dramatic emphasis.)

Think of a colon as being the two headlamps of a car, shining on to a list, a quotation, or an explanation!

Insert a colon in each sentence where appropriate.

Indicate in the brackets provided whether it introduces a list (L), a quotation (Q) or an explanation (E). Note that there is a space after the colon, but not before it.

> **TIP:**
>
> Read the example aloud to hear where you take a pause.

I am proactive in my personal development my most recent qualification was achieved through the Northern Council for Further Education (NCFE). ( )

Some individuals have serious and/or multiple needs, which can affect all areas of their lives social, psychological, emotional, physical, intellectual, and spiritual. ( )

In the fashion industry, there are two distinctive paths for sustainability in material reuse recycle and upcycle. ( )

Marilyn Monroe was attributed with saying the following "Give a girl the right shoes, and she can conquer the world." ( )

The team working in partnership is essential to support the critical principle of information-sharing, which should be proportionate, necessary, relevant, accurate, timely, and secure. ( )

Each jacket I upcycled was a different size, so the panels in the backs were different some of the jackets had thin panels in the back and others had wide. ( )

✓ Compare your answers with those in the 'Corrected versions' on page 216.

Semicolons

1. Semicolons divide statements that are closely related

The semicolon acts like the wall between semi-detached houses. You have two homes within one big building. A semicolon divides two sentences, but they are attached to each other in meaning, so it is worth using a semicolon to divide them, rather than a full stop.

Note that the second sentence begins with a lower-case letter, as in the following example:

> The semicolon looks like a full stop on top of a comma; it acts like a full stop.

2. Semicolons link equal or short statements

> United we stand; divided we fall.
>
> I called on you; you were out.

You could link the statements with 'but'. Instead, we can use a semicolon.

Note that if the second sentence begins with 'and', that would be an improper sentence, so a semicolon is not used.

In the sentence below, the semicolon replaces a link word, like 'so'.

> It is a lovely day; I think I will go for a walk.

3. Semicolons divide phrases in a list

If you have a list of single items, a comma is enough to separate them, as follows:

> Holiday packing list: passport, money, tickets, books, sunhat etc.

However, if you have a list of phrases (still introduced by a colon), it can be confusing just to use commas, so we clearly separate phrases with semicolons, thus:

Holiday packing list: all family passports; money, including English pounds and American dollars; tickets for the flight, but also for the train to the airport; books and magazines, preferably lightweight; sunhats and sun creams; suitcase with enough clothes for the beach, rainy days, warm days and evenings out; and appropriate footwear, such as trainers, flipflops and evening shoes.

Note that we still use a semicolon before the final phrase which is linked to the previous ones with 'and'.

4. Semicolons also divide multiple references in an in-text citation:

Studies which have focused on this phenomenon, rather than the effect of it on diabetic women, have been performed predominantly in Australia (Brisbane & Giglia, 2013; Connolly et al., 2019).

Divide each of the following statements with a semicolon:

Cut the passing thread so that two pieces are laid over the felt each end should have a large tail.

Use waxed thread and sew the two passing threads down each stitch should be around 4 mm apart.

Corporate events are run by organisations they can be for a variety of audiences.

Security is especially important when you are running events where children are in attendance you may need an added form of security protection if there are celebrities, politicians, or anyone in the public eye at the event.

Integrated working is to provide unified support to service users with multiple and complex needs it is used as a preventative and early intervention method, as it reduces risk factors that contribute to a poor outcome for children and young people.

Put a colon and semicolons into each of these sentences, replacing commas where necessary:

I was provided with training in four areas Introduction to care, moving and handling, first aid, and medication.

Some individuals have serious and/or multiple needs that can affect all areas of their lives social, psychological, emotional, physical, intellectual, and spiritual they challenge us as caregivers to provide responsive solutions.

With the planning for any event, the fundamentals are very similar, find out the purpose of the event and plan the event accordingly, choose an appropriate venue, produce a relevant theme, invite the target audience, have a project plan and itinerary, and keep within budget.

The areas I feel I could improve whilst on placement are firstly, setting small, manageable, and achievable goals to improve my learning in a specific timeframe, secondly, prioritise tasks through the day and thirdly, achieve a good work-life balance.

The wedding planner's duties will include managing the guest logistics, working with the venue/s, managing external staff, as well as internal staff, meet any external suppliers and manage their deliveries and simply ensure that the wedding goes exactly to plan. (5 duties)

This is a particularly complex example, so take your time with this!

> **TIP:**
>
> Make sure you find FIVE Wembley-based Facebook groups (not six) and separate them with semicolons.

The author attempted to contact eight resident associations from areas in Brent, because residents' associations are typically heavily involved in local issues, and five Wembley-based Facebook groups, friends of Eton Grove Park, Quintain Living Wembley Residents Group, What's happening on Preston Road, Wembley Park, 'All things in Wembley, local info, selling, services, and more…' and 'You know you come from Wembley if…'.

Revision challenge

▶ **Insert one colon and three semicolons in this passage so that it is a list of factors introduced by a colon, with each factor separated by a semicolon.**

When choosing a conference venue, there are three important factors that need to be taken into consideration. The venue must meet the needs of the conference, including providing the presenters with the correct equipment, and the delegates with suitable catering, rooms, seating, lighting, materials etc. The venue must be of the right capacity for the event and contain the correct number of break-out rooms, which will need to be set up according to the client's preferred layout. The location of the venue is critical, as it will need to have good transport links to open the event up to delegates from across the country.

✓ Compare your answers with those in the 'Corrected versions' on pages 216-218.

Dots and Dashes

Dots

Three dots (ellipsis) add drama when a sentence tails off.

> The murderer was about to strike…

They can also show where there are missing words in a quotation, or missing sections in a passage.

> Anna's medical knowledge of type-2 diabetes is poor, which is demonstrated when she asks when she should take insulin: "…first thing in the morning, before a meal, two hours after a meal, before driving, at bedtime, when the moon is full, on dustbin day?"

Dashes

Dashes can also add drama! Note they have <u>a space on either side</u>, which differentiates them from a hyphen that has no space on either side.

> Space – the final frontier!

They also point (like an arrow) to what is following, instead of using a colon.

> Still images are everywhere, and they all have different objectives – to advertise, inform, educate, persuade, and entertain.

> I was about to face my toughest challenge yet – an undergraduate degree.

You can often choose between a dash or a colon. Take the sentence below.

> The loop for the back of the jacket had two sewing options visible stitching or invisible stitching.

You could decide to 'shine headlights' on the options, with a colon.

> The loop for the back of the jacket had two sewing options: visible stitching or invisible stitching.

OR you could point to the options with an 'arrow'.

> The loop for the back of the jacket had two sewing options – visible stitching or invisible stitching.

Either is perfectly acceptable.

References in order of appearance, as supplied by the student authors:

Brisbane, J.M. & Giglia, R.C. (2013, October 23). Experiences of expressing and storing colostrum antenatally: A qualitative study of mothers in regional Western Australia.
Journal of Child Health Care. 2015; 19: 206–215 https://doi.org/10.1177/1367493513503586

Connolly, E.L., Reinkowsky, M., Giglia, R., Sexton, B., Lyons-Wall, P., Lo, J., & O'Sullivan, T.A. (2019). Education on antenatal colostrum expression and the Baby Friendly Health Initiative in an Australian hospital: An audit of birth and breastfeeding outcomes. Breastfeeding Review. 2019; 27: 21–30

Commas

Full stops end sentences. Commas are agents of separation, used to separate various features of language.

> I always smile when I hear the Christmas story read aloud, especially by children, and they read the words, "The shepherds came with haste and found, Mary, Joseph and the babe lying in a manger" (based on King James Version, Luke 2:16). Wow! That really was a king-sized manger to accommodate all three of them!
>
> To ensure it is clear that only the baby Jesus was in the manger, we put a comma between Joseph and the babe, thus: "The shepherds came with haste and found Mary, Joseph, (pause) and the babe lying in a manger."

When a comma comes after the penultimate item in a list of three or more items, as in the Bible verse above, it is called an Oxford, Harvard or serial comma. Despite being linked with Oxford, it is not used very much in English orthography. Just use it when it is necessary to clarify the sense of a sentence, by separating words appropriately, as in the story of the king-sized manger!

Many of my students tell me they were taught at primary school NOT to put a comma before 'and', so they are hesitant to begin doing so. At primary level, we write simple sentences and are taught that when we say, "I went to the shop for milk, bread and eggs," no comma is needed before the 'and', because it is clear there are three distinct items on the shopping list.

If I was asked to buy custard creams and bread and butter pudding, it is not so clear whether there are two, three or four items on the list. Is the bread separate from the butter pudding and the custard separate from the creams? 'Custard creams' are a type of biscuit, while 'bread and butter pudding' is a well-known dessert. Am I required to buy biscuits and a pudding, or custard and two types of creams (maybe pouring and ready whipped), to go with the pudding? Only the punctuation will tell me. Thus, "I bought custard, creams, and bread and butter pudding." The commas **separate** the three items.

It may be helpful to know that the word 'comma' comes from the Greek verb 'koptein', which means 'to cut' or 'separate'. So, a comma separates different items or parts of a sentence. The grammar checker on a computer will often indicate when a comma is needed to separate clauses, but what are clauses? Clauses are short sentences that stand on their own, but when they are linked with 'and', 'so' or 'but', for example, a comma is used to separate them. Look at the following example:

> I am very tired, but it is too early to go to bed.

The two clauses are: **'I am very tired,'** and **'It is too early to go to bed.'** The comma separates the two clauses, even when they have been linked with 'but'.

It is important to know that not every sentence that contains 'but' will have a comma before the 'but'. In the later section entitled 'Introductory, intermediate and following phrases', we will look at the use of commas to introduce a following phrase. The link word 'but' only has a comma before it if the following phrase could be a sentence in its own right, or if the sentence is so long that a pause is needed for breath.

For such a tiny mark, the comma has many uses. See how essential it is to put a comma in this command: **"Let's eat Dad!"** It should be punctuated, **"Let's eat, Dad!"** – to separate the command from the person you are commanding and to show that you are talking to Dad and not planning to devour him!

Similarly, who knew how dangerous it could be to see a health practitioner, according to the following sentence?

David has had many cues to action from his external environment, the first being his older brother suffering from two strokes due to his diabetes and his health practitioner, who warned him about his diet.

To make it clear that the poor health practitioner is not blamed for the stroke, we need to use a comma to separate the reason for the stroke and the second cue to action, thus:

> ✓ David has had many cues to action from his external environment, the first being his older brother suffering from two strokes due to his **diabetes, and** his health practitioner, who warned him about his diet.

Example 1

How do you read the sentence below?

If System 1 is running the outcome of typing this code will look like the image shown to the left in the red box.

The sentence could be read in two ways:

If System 1 is running, (then) the outcome of typing this code will look like the image shown to the left in the red box.

If System 1 is running the outcome of typing, (then) this code will look like the image shown to the left in the red box.

Which is correct? (Answer after the References for this section!)

In this example, the comma almost acts to replace the word 'then'.

Example 2

The most prominent of these was the dispute between his predecessor Pope Gregory VII and Henry IV the Holy Roman Emperor.

How many people was the dispute between?

Could it be four? 1) 'his predecessor' 2) Pope Gregory VII 3) Henry IV and 4) 'the Holy Roman Emperor'?

Answer: No, because the 'and' that comes before the last name in the list comes before Henry IV, **not** before the Holy Roman Emperor, so Henry IV **is** the Holy Roman Emperor and the last person mentioned. So, could the answer be three?

Out of context, we do not know if there are three people – 'his predecessor', 'Pope Gregory VII', and (the third and final contender) 'Henry IV, the Holy Roman Emperor'.

However, in the context of the essay, we are told that Pope Clement's predecessor **was** Pope Gregory, so the dispute was only between two people.

To make this clear, we could write it like this:

> The most prominent of these was the dispute between his predecessor, **who was** Pope Gregory VII, and Henry IV, **who was** the Holy Roman Emperor.

But that sounds very repetitive and, if you have a strict word count, it uses four more words than you need!

Instead, we could put brackets around the detail, like this:

> The most prominent of these was the dispute between his predecessor (Pope Gregory VII) and Henry IV (the Holy Roman Emperor).

However, brackets look rather intrusive and in an essay are usually reserved for in-text citations, so we replace the brackets with commas, thus:

> ✓ The most prominent of these was the dispute between his predecessor, Pope Gregory VII, and Henry IV, the Holy Roman Emperor.

(Note that we don't need a comma at the end of the sentence because of the full stop there anyway.)

In this example, the comma replaces the words 'who was'.

To practice using commas with names, look at Chapter 1.

Example 3

Which comma needs to be removed from the sentence below?

The chosen method or tool proposed to conduct this research, will be semi-structured interviews, enabling the researcher to combine the positive aspects of both structured and unstructured interview techniques.

Answer: The verb should not be separated from its subject. You would never say "I (breath) went shopping today." Therefore, no comma is needed between the subject of the sentence, *"The chosen method or tool proposed to conduct this research..."* and its verb, *"will be..."*

However, if the sentence had an intermediate phrase inserted, as below, you would put commas around the intermediate phrase, as though putting it in brackets:

The chosen method or tool proposed to conduct this research, as suggested by the University, will be semi-structured interviews.

The second comma is correctly used in the full example above, before 'enabling'.

See the teaching pages on 'Introductory, intermediate and following phrases' (from page 167), with numerous sentences in which to practise using commas to separate phrases.

Example 4

Findings suggest that verbal working memory can be positively associated with academic performance, and trait anxiety can be slightly associated with verbal working memory (Owens et al., 2008).

Here, the comma acts as the anchoring foot of an old-fashioned pair of weighing scales, with the pans balancing on either side. The sentence above comprises two sentences:

1. Findings suggest that verbal working memory can be positively associated with academic performance.

2. Trait anxiety can be slightly associated with verbal working memory.

The sentences have been linked with 'and', but the comma is needed to clarify the sense. Without a comma, the sentence suggests that 'working memory can be positively associated with [both] academic performance and trait anxiety.'

The comma is critical to make it clear that 'trait anxiety' begins a balancing sentence.

Example 5

In the sentence below, the comma is again critical for the sense:

Since Nicklinson proposed amendments to the Suicide Act 1961 (to permit physician-assisted suicide for terminally ill patients) have been unsuccessfully considered by both the House of Lords and the House of Commons.

At first glance, it looks as though we have an introductory phrase indicating that Nicklinson proposed amendments to the Suicide Act 1961. However, the rest of the sentence does not follow, and there is no subject to go with the verb 'have been'. In fact, the subject of the sentence is not Nicklinson, but 'proposed amendments [which]... have been unsuccessfully considered...' Nicklinson is actually the name of a law case. Inserting the comma makes this clear:

> ✓ Since [the case of] Nicklinson, proposed amendments to the Suicide Act 1961 (to permit physician-assisted suicide for terminally ill patients) have been unsuccessfully considered by both the House of Lords and the House of Commons.

Insert commas where appropriate in the sentences below:

> ***TIP:***
>
> Read the sentences aloud to hear where you need to pause for breath or to make the sense clear. If you are not sure, take an exaggerated breath where you think there might be a comma and see whether that still makes sense.

Steph stated that she is working towards a community detox with her keyworker and her keyworker has advised she will be prescribed Thiamine Hydrochloride. **(1 comma needed)**

To reflect his status, the landowner's clothes are made from good quality fabrics, such as his waxed cotton dungarees, lined with sheepskin and his waterproof animal hide coat. **(1 comma needed)**

Vygotsky's (1978) theory of child development can be used to understand the psychological components influencing the child-teacher relationship and how this relationship can affect the development of the child. **(1 comma needed)**

The author defines the evidence-based approach to improve decision-making and the use of evidence is more effective than subjective hunches. **(1 comma needed)**

The Barça Innovation Hub has a 'Robot Pol'. This enabled children to visit Camp Nou, using a remote-controlled robot and a 16-year-old was also visited by one of the players. **(1 comma needed)**

> The article utilized the following parameters* to analyse whether an area is at risk of or undergoing gentrification: household income housing prices % of renters % of non-white % of higher education and housing affordability.
>
> *Tip: There should be five commas to separate the six parameters!

In this example, you could use semicolons instead of commas to separate the parameters in the list. See the teaching pages on 'Colons and Semicolons, Dots and Dashes' (from page 128).

> A survey demonstrated that of the 56 maternity units within the UK that responded 73% offered colostrum harvesting advice to diabetic women 25% offered advice to women who had risk factors while 19% offered advice to all women (Pathak, 2017).

Tip: In this sentence there could be four commas – to separate the intermediate phrase from the main sentence and between the different percentages!

> ✓ Check your answers with those in the 'Corrected versions' on page 218.

Direct Speech

Use a comma when introducing or reporting direct speech. For example:

> My tutor said, "It is really important to read the assignment brief through carefully."
>
> I retorted in no uncertain terms, "I always do!"

If the speaker is mentioned at the end or the middle of the sentence, a comma still separates the speaker from the words said:

> "Make sure you proofread your work before you hand it in," the lecturer reminded the class.
>
> "I don't know how to," muttered my friend.
>
> "In which case," I replied, "you need to get yourself a guide to proofreading!"

Note that when the spoken words are split up, as in the sentence above, a comma is needed on both sides of the speaker.

If the spoken words end in a question mark or an exclamation mark, the comma is not used:

"Watch out!" she screamed. "Why?" he yelled.

Commas in Citations and Dates

According to the APA 7th guidelines, when writing in-text citations that are in brackets, a comma separates the author from the date, e.g., (Smith & Jones, 2015). If a direct quote is used, the page number is needed, and is also separated from the date with a comma, e.g., (Black, 2020, p. 5).

However, if the citation is part of the sentence, the date is already separated from the author by the bracket, so no comma is needed:

> Smith & Jones (2015) corroborated the argument.

In Harvard referencing, no comma separates the author from the date. Page numbers follow a colon, as in (Black 2020: 5).

When you use multiple dates, put commas between them. Separate the month from the year, and the day from the month, with a comma. For example:

> The next meeting of the committee will take place on Monday, May 5th, 2021, at 7.30 p.m.

Commas in Numbers

In the UK, commas are used to break large numbers over 999 into groups of three, to make them easier to read. Thus, we write 1,000 for one thousand, 25,000 for twenty-five thousand and 1,000,000 for 1 million.

1 billion, which is one thousand million, is written 1,000,000,000.

However, years like 1812 and 2001 are NOT split into groups of 3 numbers.

Summary

Commas separate:

1. Items in a list
2. Multiple adjectives or describing words
3. Names from a detail about the person
4. Speech from the person being addressed and/or the person doing the speaking, as in, "Let's go, Philip," she said.
5. Two clauses that have been linked with a joining word (conjunction)
6. The introductory phrase from the main sentence
7. The phrase following the main sentence – often an example or an explanation that may begin with 'as', 'because' or 'which'
8. An intermediate phrase in the middle of a sentence
9. A quotation that is a full sentence from the author or the introduction (When a short quotation that is not a sentence is used as part of your writing, it does not need a comma to separate it. For example, Phillips (2010) described the capture of Jerusalem by the Crusaders in 1099 as "an astonishing achievement".)
10. The author from the date, and the date from the page number, in an in-text citation, when referencing in APA 7th style.
11. Dates and days e.g., Sunday, April 3rd, 2022
12. Numbers into groups of 3 for easier reading e.g., 1,000,000

References in order of appearance, as supplied by the student authors:

Luke 2:16 – King James Bible. https://www.kingjamesbibleonline.org › Luke-2-16

Owens, M., Stevenson, J., Norgate, R., & Hadwin, J.A. (2008) Processing efficiency theory in children: working memory as a mediator between trait anxiety and academic performance. Anxiety Stress Coping. 2008 Oct; 21(4):417–30. doi: 10.1080/10615800701847823.

R (Nicklinson) v Ministry of Justice [2014] UKSC 38

Vygotsky, L.S. (1978). *Mind in society: the development of higher psychological processes.* London: Harvard University Press.

Pathak, S. (2017) Practice of antenatal breast expression in the National Health Service in England. *International Journal of Health Research and Medical Legal Practice,* 3(1):12–14

Phillips, J. P. (2010). *Holy Warriors: a modern history of the Crusades* (1st ed.). Vintage.

✓ Example 1: Sentence 1 is correct.

First and Third Person

Any writing is from a certain point of view. In fiction, the narrator usually tells the story objectively about other people, using the **third person,** signified by the pronouns he/she/they or it and his/hers/theirs or its.

A reflective report about, for example, your experience on a work placement is written from your perspective, using I and my in the singular form or we and our in the plural form. This is written in **first person**.

The **second person** point of view is when you involve yourself in the account, by saying, for example, "You know when you have done the experiment correctly because your liquid crystallises."

An easy way to remember the three points of view is using 1, 2 and 3.

- 1st person (1) looks like I.
- 2nd person (2) rhymes with you.
- 3rd person (3) rhymes with he or she.

Academic writing is usually required to be in 3rd person. However, if you have written your assignment in 1st person, and realise at the last minute it needs to be in 3rd person, it is easy to change it.

Let's take the following example in 1st person:

> Through the data I have collected, France is the most viable country for the company to expand into.

You could just take out 'I have', leaving:

> Through the data collected, France is the most viable country for the company to expand into.

However, the sense is unclear. It would be better to slightly rephrase it, removing four words and adding one:

> ~~Through the~~ Data ~~I have~~ collected <u>suggests</u> France is the most viable country for the company to expand into.

The final version changed from 1st to 3rd person is thus:

> Data collected suggests France is the most viable country for the company to expand into.

Sometimes, phrases or sentences can be turned round.

Thus, instead of writing in the 1st person,

I will use a program like 'Otter' to transcribe interviews,

you could turn it around to put it in 3rd person and say,

A program like 'Otter' will be used to transcribe interviews.

Doing this, you change the active voice (I will use) to a passive voice (will be used).

There may be some occasions, such as in a dissertation, when you need to indicate what you plan to do. If you have been told the dissertation must be written purely in 3rd person, you can refer to yourself obliquely as 'the researcher' or 'the author' and say, "The researcher will examine the findings before offering a hypothesis for consideration."

As mentioned in the teaching page on 'Rephrasing' (page 191), there will be numerous ways a sentence can be rephrased, so there is no definitive version!

Change the following sentences from 1st person to 3rd person by rephrasing them:

In this reflection, I will be using Rolfe's structure rather than Gibbs' reflective cycle.

My findings suggest that frequent text intervention could have an impact in increasing participants' perceived severity of their condition.

I will analyse the interviews to collect data for both focus groups.

An article I came across analyses the 'still image' and opens up the mind to how there are many different variables that go into an image.

The variables are vast, so here I will name a few and discuss each individually to explain how they can change the viewer's perspective of the image.

Compare your versions with the suggestions in the 'Corrected versions' on page 219.

Homophones and Similar-Sounding Words!

There are hundreds of homophones (words which sound the same but are spelt differently) and words which are confusingly similar, but here are selected examples that feature regularly in my students' work, in alphabetical order, not order of importance.

Advise/Advice

This is the best homophone to start with, as it helps with one of the trickiest of homophones – practice/practise (see below).

You can **hear** the difference between 'advise' and 'advice'. One is a **verb** (a doing word), and one is a **noun** (the **name** of something). 'Advice' ends in a very light, soft 's' sound, like 'ice cream' and is the **name** of something that you give or receive (hopefully good!).

'Advice', then, is the **noun**, like 'ice', 'vice' and 'dice'. 'Advise', by contrast, is a **verb** or doing word, like 'recognise' and 'sympathise', all of which have a clear 'zz' sound, like a bee buzzing!

So, in your writing, listen out for the sound in the word, whether it buzzes like the verb or has a soft 's' sound like ice! You can also check whether the word is used as a noun or as a verb and you will then be able to choose the correct option in context.

Affect/Effect

This is another very common error! Once again, one is a noun, and one is a verb. 'Effect' is the noun, so you can have an effect or the effect. In the context of your writing, if you could say 'the effect' with two 'e's together, then you need the noun spelt with an 'e'. ('Effect' can also be a doing word, but is rarely used in this way, so don't worry about it!)

'Affect' is a verb and will never have 'the' or 'an' in front of it. It will have a noun in front of it that does the affecting. It may also have an indication of tense, with 'has' (affected) or 'will' (affect). Try to remember the following short sentences:

Global warming has affected the planet.

The effect of global warming is catastrophic.

Another way to remember the difference is to think of similar words that you can remember more easily. For example, 'affect' is a verb like 'affirm', while 'effect' is a noun like 'effort', where you can hear the 'e' at the beginning very clearly.

Choose one of the following to insert in the gaps in the short passages below:

affects   effect   affected   effects   affect

The theme of the G8 summit was, 'Global warming ………….. the planet.' We are all …………. in some way. To have an …………., we must all reduce our carbon footprint. Clearly…………. by the subject, the President insisted, "We must ensure the recommendations from the G8 summit take immediate ………….."

An ………….. of binge drinking is a headache! Robin had too much to drink and was badly …………. However, the …………. of taking Paracetamol is dramatic, and the medication has no side …………..

Compare your insertions with the corrected versions at the bottom of the Homophones section.

Assess/Access

The easiest way to explain this is to share the point of the double 'c' in 'access'. If you have a 'c' followed by an 'e' or an 'i', the 'c' sounds soft, as in 'ace' or 'acid'. To keep the 'c' sound hard, we must protect it from the softening power of the 'e' or 'i' by doubling the 'c'. The first 'c' is thus kept hard, while the second 'c' can sound soft, as in the words 'ac/cident', 'ac/cept', 'ac/celerate' – and, of course, 'ac/cess'.

Thus, 'assess' with no double 'c' has soft sounds in both syllables.

Asses/Assess

These terms can cause confusion, as many students do not realise that 'asses' are a form of donkey, as distinct from their intended meaning – to do with assessment!

'Es' at the end of a word usually indicates a plural (see the teaching pages on 'Plurals' from page 182) and sounds much softer, like 'iz' at the end of the word.

It is not emphasised in the way that 'assess' with the double 's' at the end is. When you have a double 's' at the end of a word, you can definitely hear it: guess, bless, digress, regress, happiness and trustworthiness.

So, in your writing, check whether you mean the plural of 'ass' or whether you are emphasising the action to 'assess'.

Bases/Basis

'Bas*es*' are the plural form of 'base', just as we saw in the example above, where 'ass*es*' is the plural form of 'ass'.

The s*i*ngular form of the term is 'bas*is*'. An alternative way to remember the spelling is to think of the question, "What **is** the bas**is** of your argument?"

Censors/Sensors

Sensors sense movement, light and heat. Censors critically examine films and books and have the power to cut offensive material out or curtail the release of a film.

Collaborate/Corroborate

These words are not homophones but are sometimes confused by my students, so are worth differentiating. The clue to the meaning of the first word and the difference from the second is 'labor', the American spelling of the English word 'labour'. It comes from the Latin – 'collaborare', which means to work ('laborare') together ('col').

While a report may talk about collaboration with colleagues, an assignment is more likely to use the word 'corroborate', which means to confirm or give support to a statement, theory or finding. As such, it is a very useful word to know.

College/Collage/Colleague

These are actually pronounced differently, so are not strictly homophones, but my students often confuse them.

> A **coll*e*ge** is a place of *e*ducation.

A **collage** is made of scraps of paper and card stuck on to a bigger piece of paper or card.

A **col<u>league</u>** is someone at work you may secretly be in <u>league</u> with to win the departmental quiz <u>league</u> each month.

Complement/Compliment

A hat that **comple**ments an outfit **complete**s it.

> I compl**i**ment you on your out**fi**t.

Thus, **comple**mentary medicine is used alongside conventional medicine to offer a more **complete** package.

Something that is compl**i**mentary is a free g**i**ft. Perhaps you could visualise being offered a compl**ime**ntary **lime** and soda on your next visit to a restaurant!

Counsel(lor)/Council(lor)

When a couns**e**llor couns**e**ls someone, they lend them a list**e**ning **e**ar and give them wis**e** advic**e**.

The homophones 'council' and 'councillor' have no 'e' in them. A counc**i**llor works for a counc**i**l and, you could say, dots the '**i**'s in local authority matters.

Deferred/Differed

The stress in these two words is in different places. In '<u>dif</u>fered', the stress is on the first syllable, as in '<u>dif</u>ferent', from which its meaning comes. 'De<u>ferred</u>', with the stress on the second syllable, comes from 'defer', which means to put off or delay. It sounds like 'preferred', which might help you to remember the correct spelling.

The ending of 'differed' reminds me of a rather painful experience! When I was a student teacher, I attended a conference on spelling. We were given a spelling test and told that it was very rare for anyone to spell the complete test correctly. Thus, the challenge was set and, as I was usually good at spelling, I was confident I would get 100%… Pride certainly came before a fall, as I spelt one of the words incorrectly! The offending word was 'benefited'. As we spell 'fitted' with two 't's, I assumed 'benefited' would also be spelt with two 't's. Alas, no! Apparently, if the stress is on the first syllable of a word with more than one syllable, there is no need to double the consonant to protect the vowel in the penultimate (last but one) syllable. The stress on the first syllable in 'di<u>ff</u>ered' means there is no need to double the 'r' before the 'ed' ending, in the same way that the stress on the first syllable in '<u>ben</u>efited' means there is no need to double the 't' before the 'ed' ending. I have never forgotten how to spell 'benefited' since!

Definitely/Defiantly

If I had £1 for every time I have seen this confusion, I would be very well off! Both words begin with 'defi'. Both words have four syllables. However, the second syllable of the first word is 'fin', while you can see 'ant' in the second word. If you need to write 'definitely', you need the one with the 'fin' and not the word with the 'ant'! Alternatively, think of this word picture to help you visualise the 'fini' in 'definitely':

de**fini**tely
finished

Discreet/Discr**ete**

If you act discreetly, you are not noticed and do not draw attention to yourself.

'Discr**e**te', on the other hand, means 'separate', as when your course consists of discr**ete** modules. It helps to remember that the version that means 'separate', separates the two 'e's with a 't'.

Dying/Dy**e**ing

This is a common error among Textiles students, who dye fabrics different colours. We usually drop the 'e' at the end of a verb when we write the 'ing' form, as when we change 'manage' to 'managing'. When we add 'ing' to 'dye', we need to keep the 'e' at the end, to differentiate it from the 'ing' form of 'die', which is 'dying'.

The reason the 'y' is used in 'dying' is because of the rule to drop the 'e' when we write the 'ing' form, which would give us 'diing'! To pronounce the word correctly, we substitute the half vowel 'y' for the 'i' and follow it with the 'ing'.

Elicit/Illicit

The 'e' at the beginning of Latin-based words is a shortened form of 'ex' and means 'out'. Thus, 'educate' means to draw out or lead out (innate knowledge etc.), as opposed to the misconception that education 'forces in' knowledge! Hence, 'e-licit' means to bring out or bring forth a response or a reaction.

Illicit, on the other hand, means illegal or unlawful.

Elude/Allude

Similarly, the 'e' in 'elude' means 'out' or 'away'. To elude someone is to evade them or escape from them, so that is the easiest way to remember the difference between 'elude' and 'allude'. Both words have the Latin 'ludere' as the root, from which we get Ludo, a game.

'Allude' has a playful meaning, as you refer to something or hint at it, without actually mentioning it!

Fazed/Phased

'Faze' is a fairly modern verb, meaning that you are put off something or daunted, whereas 'phase' is a noun that means a stage in the developmental process. The moon has different phases, while the 'terrible twos' is a phase in childhood. The way to remember the difference may be to think of 'faze' being similar to 'face'. When in a daunting situation, your face may show how fazed you are. Alternatively, remember the version that begins with 'ph' by thinking, 'Philip is going through a moody phase!'

Gauge/Gage

'Gage' is an old version of the modern, preferred spelling of 'gauge', to do with measuring and estimating. It is still sometimes used in technical and engineering fields, but 'gauge' is the recommended form in academic writing.

Insistence/Insistent

This is a common error as it is difficult to hear the endings. There are hundreds of similar examples. In many cases, as here, one is a noun, and one is a describing word (adjective). If you describe yourself as 'content', that may help you remember that the describing word is 'insis**tent**', so the noun must be spelt with a 'ce'. Myriad more familiar nouns end in '**ce**', such as 'place', 'ice', 'mince' and 'dance', so the 'ce' version of this homophone is another noun.

This may also help with **ance**/**ant** words, such as 'relev**ance**' and 'relev**ant**'. The noun version ends in '**ce**', so the adjective is relev**ant**.

Another way to remember the difference is to think that the word 'noun' has no 't' in it, whereas 'adjective' does contain a 't'. Thus, faced with a choice between 'relevant' and 'relevance', the adjective will be the one with the 't' – relevant.

Insure/Ensure

If you want to mak**e sure** of something, you **ensure** it. If you have a very valuable r**i**n**g**, it would be wise to **in**sure it!

Led/Lead

This is a tricky homophone as the past tense of the verb 'to lead' (pronounced differently – leed) is 'led'. Maybe the easiest way to remember this is to think that the past tense of most verbs ends in 'ed' (walked, edited, pruned etc.), so 'led' is the past tense of 'to lead'. 'Lead' pronounced the same way as 'led' is, of course, a metal.

Miner/Minor

A **miner** works in a **mine**. A min**or**, by contrast, is less imp**or**tant, like a min**or** issue.

Originally/Organically

These sound quite different but, because they contain so many of the same letters, they are often confused. They are both five syllables long, begin with 'or' and end in 'ally', but if you separate the syllables, you can hear the difference.

One contains 'gin'! The other contains 'organ'.

If you are describing something as 'organic' or growing 'organically', be sure to choose the spelling with 'organ' in it. Otherwise, if the root of the word you require is 'origin', look for the word containing 'gin'!

Palate/Pallet/Palette

My art students nearly always trip up on this homophone. They need to use the artist's colour palette, which is a French word, as signified by the feminine 'ette' ending. Think of the artists sitting in Montmartre in Paris to help you visualise the correct spelling. Other French words we have adopted, like 'brunette' and 'layette', or names, like Annette and Lynette, may also help you remember the correct ending.

A typical pallet with a double 'll' is a structure usually made of planks of wood side by side (like the 'll') and used to transport items. While it can be made of other materials, visualise a pallet made of wooden planks to convey the spelling with the 'll' side by side.

The final version – palate – refers to the roof of the mouth. One way to remember this is to think: "The toffee I ate stuck to my palate!"

Poses/Possess

Like 'Asses/Assess', the distinction between 'poses' and 'possess' lies in the emphasis the double 's' gives to the word. As in 'asses', the 'es' sounds like 'iz' at the end of the word. Where 'asses' is a noun, 'poses' is a verb. This is the third person form of the verb 'to pose' and is the only person in a verb to have an 's' at the end of it. See the 'Agreement of verbs' teaching page (page 108), with the mnemonic: "Single subject – s on the verb!"

Here we have two similarly spelt verbs but with very different pronunciations and meanings. 'Poses' sounds like 'roses' with the emphasis on its long 'o' sound, whereas 'possess' has its emphasis on 'ess' in the second syllable. In your writing, check which of the two verbs you need, according to its pronunciation and the meaning of the word – whether you mean a) poses a question or stands in a certain way or b) possess, which means 'to own'.

Practice/Practise

This is one of the trickiest homophones I know, but I tackle it with reference to the first homophone in this list – 'Advice/Advise', where at least you can hear the difference between the two words. In just the same way, 'practice' with a 'c' is the noun and 'practise' with an 's' is the verb.

Practise (verb)   Advise

Practice (noun)   **Advice**

For the visual learners among you, it may be helpful to visualise the sea-blue verb 'practise' and associate the 'se' ending with seeing the sea.

Similarly, visualise the cherry-red noun 'practice' with the cherry-red 'ce' ending.

Insert the correct homophone in the sentences below:

I must do my piano …………

I ………….d really hard.

The doctor's ………….. is just down the street.

In …………., the NHS does a wonderful job.

Mollie …………s mindfulness techniques.

> **TIP:**
>
> If you could add the 'ed' ending to the practise/practice choice, then it will be the past tense of the verb, so choose 'practise'. This may help when deciding which version to use in the fourth sentence above!

Compare your insertions with the corrected versions at the bottom of the Homophones section.

Precede/Proceed

'Pre' means 'before' and is a prefix that goes before or in front of a word. 'Cede' comes from the Latin 'cedere', meaning 'to go'. Thus, if Prince William 'precedes' Prince Harry, he goes before Prince Harry in the line of succession.

'Pro' is a Latin prefix that means 'forward'. The 'ceed' again comes from the Latin 'cedere', but over time the spelling has changed from 'cede' to 'ceed'. Thus, 'proceed' literally means 'go forward' or 'travel onwards' and gives rise to words like 'procession', a group of people moving forwards, and the 'proceeds' of a sale – cash flow resulting from the sale.

Precedent/President

A helpful rule to know is that the hard 'c' sound goes soft like 's' when followed by an 'e' or an 'i', as in 'city centre'. It also happens with the half-vowel 'y', as in 'cycle'.

When followed by an 'e', an 'i' or a 'y', the same happens with the hard 'g' sound, softening to a 'j', as in 'ginger' and 'gyrate'. Incidentally, that is why some words beginning with 'g' have a 'u' next to it to keep the following 'e', 'i' or 'y' from softening the 'g', as in 'guess', 'guitar' and 'guy'.

Applying the soft 'c' rule, we can hear the soft 'c' in 'precedent', which is a noun stemming from the verb to 'precede' which, as we saw in '**Pre**cede/**Pro**ceed', comes from the Latin, meaning 'to go before'. Thus, a '**pre**cedent' is something that happened before or earlier and gives us an example or rule to follow.

No soft 'c' can be heard in 'president', which has a definite buzzing 's' sound. Interestingly, President Biden's surname is almost found in the word 'president'!

Principle/Principal

One of these is like a rule and one is a person. The version ending in 'le', 'princip**le**', is the ru**le**, which also ends in '**le**'. That means that 'princi**pal**' is a person, like a pal. You could remember it by thinking, "My Pa's pal is princi**pal** of this College."

Quite/Quiet

Knowledge of the cute but rather old-fashioned 'magic e' rule helps here. Without an 'e', 'quit' has a short 'i' vowel. 'Magic e' changes the vowel sound to become long, so it says 'quite'. This is quite distinct from the 2-syllable word 'qui –et'. To remember to keep the 'et' together in 'quiet', you could think, "ET is quiet!"

Queue/Cue

The British are renowned for loving queues! The French word of the same spelling means 'tail'. So, a 'queue' is a long tail out of a shop! Say the letters of the word in a rhythmic way – q, ue, ue, to help you spell it.

A 'cue' is a signal to do something. In the context of your work, decide whether the word required is a signal or a line of people.

Rational/Rationale

This is a very common error among my students. They are required to give a rationale for their dissertation or coursework. As with many homophones, the clue to their difference lies in the ending. The word 'rational' ends in 'al', which is typical of adjectives or describing words, such as 'final', 'casual', 'musical' and 'beneficial'. So, you might have a rational argument.

A 'rationale' with an 'e' is a reason or justification for doing something, which is why it is used to introduce academic pieces of work.

Roll/Role

While there are many uses for the word 'roll', whether as a noun (bread roll, roll of wallpaper or being on a roll when you are having good fortune) or as a verb (roll the parchment up into a scroll or roll the ball down the bowling alley), there is only one use for the word 'role', which means a part you play. In academic writing, it is more likely you would be talking about a role model or a role played by something or someone, but check the meaning to be sure.

Salvage/Selvedge

This is an easy one to remember as 'selvedge' is the 'edge' of a piece of material that is tightly woven to stop the edge fraying. 'Salvage' comes from saving or rescuing, so an aeroplane's black box might be salvaged from the wreckage after a crash.

Stationery/Stationary

One of these is a noun (name), while the other is an adjective (describing word). Fortunately, the adjective contains the 'a'! For example, "The train was stationary." (The 'a' in 'train' may also help you remember the 'a' in the adjective used to describe the train.)

On the other hand, "A letter is an example of stationery."

They're/There/Their

These homophones are such common pitfalls, especially 'there' and 'their'. All begin with 'the'. The word with the apostrophe signifies a letter has been pushed out, so they're is the contraction of 'they are', as in:

"Looking at the England footballers – they're a great squad!"

All the words of place (here, there and where) contain the root 'here', so the word that denotes a place or a fact is 'there'. Examples are:

The ball landed over there. (Word of place)

There are hundreds of stars in the sky. (Fact)

It is easier to remember the final 'their' if you think of the phrase "Their eyes (i) are (r) blue", because the 'i' and the 'r' come in the right order after 'the'.

Another way to remember 'their' is that it is the only one of the three homophones that looks as though it contains a person (i) with a body and a head, so anything that belongs to a person is 'theirs', with the person (i) in the word!

To/Too/Two

'To' has a short sound, so is the shortest of the three words.

'Too' sounds like the number 'two', so it has two 'o's which add emphasis to the word, whether you use it in a sentence like "This cake is too delicious for words!" or "I'm going shopping; do you want to come too?"

The 'w' in the number 'two' is easy to remember if you think of the related words: 'twins', 'twice', 'twelve' and 'twenty'.

Underlining/Underlying

These are not real homophones, of course, because the words sound different when enunciated clearly. However, they are so similar that they are sometimes confused. When someone talks about an underlying issue, this may be misheard as underlining. An underlying issue may be hidden, whereas underlining something emphasises it and draws attention to it. So, in your writing, check whether something is lying underneath where it might be hidden, or whether it is obvious because you have underlined it.

Varies/Various

Again, these are not really homophones because the words are pronounced differently. 'Varies' has two syllables and is the third person form of the verb 'to vary'. 'Various', on the other hand, has three syllables and is a describing word or adjective. Slowly enunciating the syllables 'va-ri-ous' and remembering the common 'ous' ending can help to distinguish between the two, when you are writing.

Where/Wear/Were

In some dialects, 'where' is pronounced like 'were', which makes this a triple homophone. In other accents, 'were' has a definite 'wurr' sound, pronounced through almost square-shaped lips, whereas the mouth is widened to pronounce 'where'. Although we can use 'were' to begin a question, it is more often used in a statement of fact, as in: "There were books and papers all over the desk." 'Were' comes from the past tense of the verb 'to be': I was, you were, they were etc. Thus, if the word you require is a vERb, use 'wERe'. We never, ever write 'There where…'!

'Where' is one of the six question words that begin with 'wh', which is another helpful aid to remembering the correct spelling. It is also a word of place, like 'there' (see 'They're/There and Their') and you can see the root word 'here' in it. So, if the word you require is to do with place, use 'where', as in: "The spot where the treasure was buried was marked with an X on the map."

Finally, remember the spelling of 'wear' in the context of wearing something, as in: "I wear earrings."

Excited/Exited

It is helpful to discuss these words, which are confusable but not strictly homophones, by discussing them in the present tense without the 'ed' ending. 'Exit', whether a noun or a verb, has a short 'i' sound, whereas 'excite' has a long 'i' sound, because of the effect of the 'magic e' (see 'Quite/Quiet'). So, when choosing which word to use, listen out for whether you need a short or a long 'i' sound.

As for which word contains the 'c', either think that the word 'Exit' needs to be as short as possible to fit on signs and/or that children get excited at Christmas!

Your/You're/Yore

The last of these three homophones is rarely used nowadays, but yore means 'long ago'. As a child, I remember learning the poem by William Makepeace Thackeray that begins:

> "There lived a sage in days of yore
> And he a handsome pigtail wore;
> But wondered much and sorrowed more
> Because it hung behind him."

You're with its apostrophe is clearly a contraction, so we can easily see that it means you are. Finally, your must belong to you.

Corrected versions

Affect/Effect

The theme of the G8 summit was, 'Global warming affects the planet.' We are all affected in some way. To have an effect we must all reduce our carbon footprint. Clearly affected by the subject, the President insisted, "We must ensure the recommendations from the G8 summit take immediate effect."

An effect of binge drinking is a headache! Robin had too much to drink and was badly affected. However, the effect of taking Paracetamol is dramatic and the medication has no side effects.

Practice/Practise

> I must do my piano practice.
>
> I practised really hard.
>
> The doctor's practice is just down the street.
>
> In practice, the NHS does a wonderful job.
>
> Mollie practises mindfulness techniques.

Hyphens

We often use two (and occasionally three) words to make one compound describing word (adjective) in front of a noun (a person, place or thing), so we put a hyphen between them to join them. For example, we talk about 'user-friendly instructions' or having 'high-maintenance lifestyles'.

If the 'compound' adjective comes BEFORE the noun, it is hyphenated, as in an up-to-date bulletin, but if the description comes AFTER the noun, the bulletin is up to date (with no hyphens).

TIP:

If you are not sure where to put hyphens, look for a noun, like 'book' or 'jumper', and check whether two words are used to make one compound adjective in front of the noun to describe it, like a dog-eared book or a cherry-red jumper.

Insert a hyphen where one is needed in these sentences.

Remember that if the noun comes **after** the describing words, **no** hyphen is needed:

Midwifery is a research informed profession.

Evidence based practice is embraced internationally as the ideal approach to improving healthcare outcomes.

The study used in depth interviews and a qualitative analysis method to determine themes.

The government's aim is to become a smoke free society within the next five years.

Occasionally, I use rather long winded sentences, so I was encouraged to condense them.

Stitching by hand was considerably more time consuming but was more effective.

According to woman centred care, the plan given to a woman is tailored to her needs.

A long term study was recommended, using historical records.

These select individuals have openly shared that they like to invest their money in quality driven, innovative designs.

The brand plans to launch their first pop up store in London within one year of launching.

The brand also aims to secure UK concessions in high end department stores, as mentioned in the brand's objectives.

The brand's consumers always have the assurance that they will be investing in products which are fashionable and on trend.

✓ Compare your answers with those in the 'Corrected versions' from page 219.

Exception to the rule:

When the first of the two words you want to join ends in 'ly', **no** hyphen joins them, as in: newly emerging technology, a highly motivated manager, and politically sensitive material.

▶ More than one hyphen is needed in these sentences!

One to one, semi structured interviews will be used to obtain rich data.

Diet education will inform Ben about food alternatives he can eat that won't increase his blood glucose levels, such as sugar free and low sugar alternatives.

It is important to have a pre event briefing with all the participants, as it ensures a smooth running and well organised event.

The teams and organisations can promote anti oppressive and anti discriminatory practices, by allowing individuals to take control of their affairs, support organisations, and employ a strengths based approach that allows people to manage their data.

With the expansion of the Metropolitan Railway in 1863, people were able to trade the rat ridden, disease infested streets of central London for healthy countryside.

From this, it can be inferred that whilst cross cultural research is being conducted, there is yet to be a time efficient, cost effective way of conducting such research.

The book is set in a post apocalyptic future, with sub zero temperatures in a life threatening environment.

Another important change in land use is the stark increase of high rise housing, due to a regeneration plan to build over 6,000 homes, as part of what aims to be the largest single site, purpose built, build to rent development anywhere in the UK. (5 to find!)

The company is positioned at the low end of the luxury market. Figure 6 shows the company against key, competing brands, ranging from the low end market to the high end market.

✓ Compare your answers with those in the 'Corrected versions' on page 220.

It is not just compound **adjectives** that can be hyphenated, but compound **nouns** as well. Thus, we have brother-in-law, Colonel-in-chief and jack-of-all-trades.

When a Christian name or a surname is made up of two proper nouns, they are hyphenated to show that they are meant to be together and are not separate names. Thus, Amelia-Rose is a Christian name, whereas Amelia Rose Jones suggests Amelia's middle name is Rose.

If compound numbers are written as words, hyphens join them, as in fifty-five and twenty-one. If an age acts as or precedes a noun, hyphens are used, as in a three-year-old and an 18-year-old student.

When verbs are combined with prepositions, they are hyphenated: check-in, make-up, and take-out.

However, when the preposition comes first, no hyphen is used: uproar, output, and underpass. In the same way, prepositions that come before a noun are not hyphenated either: outpatient, offspring and indoors.

Increasingly in English, hyphens are being dropped after prefixes, so that we write readjust, predispose and antihero. However, where two of the same letters are juxtaposed, as in co-operate, pre-empt, non-negotiable and re-evaluate, a hyphen makes the word easier to read.

Similarly, it can be easier to read compound words like multi-disciplinary if a hyphen is used, but the rules are changing and multidisciplinary is now the accepted form, although I doubt tutors would cross out the hyphen if you inserted one in your work.

A hyphen can also clarify the meaning of a word. 'Re-sent', as in 'sent again', has a totally different meaning to 'resent' – 'feel bitter about', while to 're-cover' a chair is not the same as to 'recover' from an illness.

As in all subjects, change takes place in language and words evolve. For an appropriate example, 'proofreading' was originally written as two words – 'proof reading'. It then became hyphenated – 'proof-reading'. It is now written 'proofreading'.

Please note that US English and British English follow different rules where hyphens are concerned!

Another exception to the rule:

In APA style, compound words beginning with 'self' are hyphenated, as in 'self-esteem' (noun), 'self-identify' (verb) and 'self-conscious' (adjective).

Insert hyphens where appropriate in these sentences:

The ring had a mother of pearl stone.

My dad built a lean to on the side of the house.

The dancer had dramatic make up.

My brother left his comrades in arms back in Iraq.

Pre war council houses are currently being refurbished.

The build up to the release of the last Harry Potter film was captivating.

Andrew Lloyd Webber has written so many beautiful musicals.

Many of the steel producing plants in Sheffield closed in the 1970s.

Three times Wimbledon champion, Boris Becker, commentated on the match.

A well thought out plan makes writing a cohesive essay much easier.

Tracy Ann Oberman starred in the sitcom, *Friday Night Dinner*, for ten years.

I was glad of my third party insurance after I bumped into another car.

'Seventy six Trombones' is the signature song in the musical, *The Music Man*.

A one day old baby was found on the steps of the Public Library.

Midwives carry out post natal checks on all new mums.

The poet, Cecil Day Lewis, also wrote mystery stories under the pseudonym, Nicholas Blake.

A red haired, ten year old girl is required for the main role in *Annie*. **(2 sets to find)**

The anti abortion campaigners filmed a pro life documentary. **(2 sets to find)**

✓ Compare your answers with those in the 'Corrected versions' on page 221.

Introductory, Intermediate and Following Phrases

Introductory Words and Phrases

Introductory **words** include useful link words, like 'Therefore', 'Consequently', 'However' and 'Furthermore', which are always followed by a comma to separate them from the rest of the sentence.

> I am on a diet. Therefore, I have given up puddings.

You can also have introductory **phrases**, which usually set the scene or give a detail. They are also separated from the rest of the sentence by a comma.

> According to the weather forecast, it will be raining tomorrow.
>
> In the recent heatwave, sales of ice cream soared.
>
> When starting university, I was concerned about note-taking during lectures.

Note how **dates** are punctuated with two commas in the sentence below.

> On September 3rd, 1939, World War II began.

✏️ Insert commas after the introductory words and phrases in each sentence below, then check the 'Corrected version' on page 222.

> According to experts the life cycle of Magellanic penguins follows a certain pattern. In September the penguins return to their nests. In October the female lays two eggs. In November the eggs are incubated for 40 days. Initially the female looks after the eggs while the male hunts for food. When hatched in December or January the parents take it in turns to look after the young. During this time the other parent searches for food in the sea (blogpatagonia.australis.com, 2017).

Sometimes, introductory phrases can be very long, so it is hard to see where the comma is needed. If this is the case, look for the subject of a sentence and its verb, usually found next to the subject. (Note: the subject of a sentence does not mean the topic of the sentence; it is the person, place or thing that is doing or being. A verb is a doing or being word.) Anything that precedes the subject is the introductory phrase. Look at the following sentence:

> To gain a better understanding of my strengths and weaknesses as a leader I first need to identify my leadership style.

> Questions: Who or what is the subject of the sentence and what is the verb near or next to it?

> Answer: I (first) need…

Thus, anything that comes before the subject (in this case – 'I') is the introductory phrase that gives a detail or, in this case, a reason. It should be separated from the main sentence that begins with the subject by a comma:

> ✓ To gain a better understanding of my strengths and weaknesses as a leader, I first need to identify my leadership style.

Look for the subject of the following sentence and separate it from the introductory phrase with a comma:

> Having taken two leadership style questionnaires I was able to find out that I am a democratic leader.

The subject of the sentence is 'I' again and this time the verb is next to it – 'was'. The comma, therefore, goes before the 'I'.

> ✓ Having taken two leadership style questionnaires, I was able to find out that I am a democratic leader.

Sentences have myriad different subjects! However, in the following paragraph, the subject of every sentence except one is 'I'.

✏️ Insert commas to separate the introductory phrase from the main sentence, then check the 'Corrected version' on page 222.

> Early on I was nominated as the team leader who would coordinate the discussions, set up meetings on Teams, and bring the slides together to form the presentation. At the start I was worried about taking on the leadership role, but was happy to do so, as I was able to make sure everyone took part. After the presentation I received positive feedback from the group about my leadership skills. However I found that I try to make everyone happy to avoid conflict. Within social work there will be conflict and challenge at times, when I will need to become assertive.

Following Phrases

> **'Ing' words** often indicate an introductory or following phrase.
>
> In the Penguin passage above, underline the two examples of **'ing' words**.
>
> In the sentence below, the **'ing' word** introduces a following phrase, which is separated from the rest of the sentence by a comma.
>
>> The method proposed to conduct this research will be semi-structured interviews, enabling the researcher to combine the positive aspects of both structured and unstructured interview techniques.
>
> The sentence could have ended at the comma, but more detail has been added in the following phrase.

A following phrase follows a comma.

✏️ **Insert commas between the main sentence and the following phrase in the sentences below:**

Figure 6 shows the brand's performance against competing brands ranging from the low-end market to the high-end market.

There is a focus on innovative procedures providing newly emerging technologies to customers.

I will create a self-development plan focusing on myself as a learner, professional, teacher, and member of a team.

I have created a SNOB analysis outlining my personal strengths, needs, opportunities and barriers.

Students are bound to have anxieties at the beginning of their university experience including finding their way around the campus, managing coursework, and achieving a good work-life balance.

On other occasions, following phrases may begin with 'as', 'because' or 'which'. They sometimes have other words in front of them, like 'such as' and 'possibly because'.

> The brand also aims to secure UK concessions in high-end department stores, as mentioned in the brand's objectives.

> The brand's consumers always have assurance they will be investing in quality-driven products, which are fashionable and on trend.

> **TIP:**
>
> In the examples above, the sentence could end where the comma is, but it goes on to add a detail in the following phrase, following a comma.

In these examples, insert a comma before the start of the following phrase, and then highlight the word which follows the comma:

> The brand uses recognisable, brown, recycled packaging which is seen throughout the brand's e-commerce packaging, in-store packaging, swing tags and branding.

> Peters et al. (2013) claim younger nurses are reported to consistently have a stronger fear of death because they may not be experienced or well-skilled in dealing with the emotional side of the experience.

> The reason I performed this section in multiple steps was so that I could understand and see what else resided within each directory as well as show other steps which have been performed.

Watch out for different words to introduce the following phrase in the sentences below, but continue to highlight the word which follows the comma:

> McAllister (2013) states resilience strategies are integral to nursing practice due to assisting patients and families to cope with many types of adversity.

> Five different locations will be compared to show the reader the changes over time with secondary research used to give more detail about the changes.

> The study found over 20% of participants experienced the floor effect so there is very little variance in the results.

To consolidate your knowledge of words that typically introduce a following phrase, write out all the words you highlighted:

....

....

....

....

....

✓ **Compare your answers with those in the 'Corrected versions' on pages 222 and 223.**

Intermediate Phrases

These are phrases (or sometimes single words) that are inserted into the middle of a sentence.

> **Example 1:**
>
> Confidentiality reasons, therefore, prevent the court from revealing the name of the young offender.

In the context of the explanation, 'therefore' could have begun the sentence with just one comma after it, but it can also be inserted in the middle of the sentence. Other single words, such as 'however', could have been used in the same way. Usually, 'therefore' is separated for emphasis or because it acts as an aside, so has commas on either side of it. However, it can sometimes be read as part of the sentence with no pause, in which case it does not need commas around it.

Consider this example:

> I have been late for work twice this week. I will therefore become more disciplined about getting up on time.

Inserting commas around 'therefore' in this example would interrupt the flow of your resolve. It is part of the sentence, not an additional extra.

If you are not sure how to punctuate a sentence with 'therefore' in the middle, read it aloud, as though to a large lecture room, projecting your voice so that people at the back can hear you. If you drop the tone of your voice when you read 'therefore', or emphasise the word, put commas around it, but if you read the sentence in the same tone, with no emphasis or pause, do not put commas around 'therefore'.

> **Example 2:**
>
> My sister has red hair like my mother. My brother, on the other hand, has brown hair like my father.

Here, 'on the other hand' could have begun the sentence as an introductory phrase, but it is inserted into the middle as an intermediate phrase, with commas around it.

> **TIP:**
>
> Usually, if punctuated correctly, you can leave out an intermediate phrase and the sentence will still make sense!

Try it with the TIP sentence above!

✏️ **Put commas around the intermediate words and phrases in the sentences below:**

The main role of the social worker however is to care for people.

It is important therefore to keep an eye on your word count for an essay, so that you do not have to go back and prune it!

Semicolons have a different function incidentally from colons and dashes.

The easiest way to proofread your work is to read it aloud as though to a packed lecture room and punctuate your pauses for breath.

Firstly using an article from the Sports Illustrator a specific case study will be analysed.

The girl dashed out of the building and running hurriedly to her car slipped on some ice.

Start in the middle and as the stitches move outwards cut away the centre bottom string.

The motives behind drinking alcohol are multifactorial and although alcohol may provide a short-term solution it can contribute to disease and premature death in the long term.

Common 'clue' words at the beginning of intermediate phrases include 'as', 'although' and 'despite'.

✓ Compare your answers with those in the 'Corrected versions' on pages 223 and 224.

> **TIP:**
>
> Press Control + F (meaning Find) or the Replace feature on the tool bar to highlight the words 'as', 'because', 'which', and other 'clue' words in your work, so that you can check whether a comma has been, or needs to be, inserted!
>
> However, be aware that this feature finds words within words, so if you type in 'as', words containing 'as' will also be highlighted!

Challenge 1

Where would you put commas in the sentence below?

> In the worst-case scenario this can lead to attendees pushing to get nearer to the front of the stage resulting in crushing and overcrowding.

Let's break this down into the component parts of the sentence, and separate the parts from each other with a comma:

<u>Introductory phrase</u>, which provides the detail or the setting,

> In the worst-case scenario,

<u>Main sentence</u>

> this can lead to attendees pushing to get nearer to the front of the stage,

It could finish here with a full stop, but you are adding more detail, so you use a comma.

<u>Following phrase</u>

> resulting in crushing and overcrowding.

Note the 'ing' verb 'resulting', which suggests a following phrase that adds more detail.

Thus, the sentence should be punctuated as follows:

✓ **In the worst-case scenario, this can lead to attendees pushing to get nearer to the front of the stage, resulting in crushing and overcrowding.**

Challenge 2

Is the punctuation correct in the sentence below?

> As there is currently no single definition of 'complex needs'; although the term is frequently used within nursing and learning disability, this assignment will use a working definition.

Using a semicolon suggests that it divides two sentences, but **As there is currently no single definition of 'complex needs';** is not a sentence.

What we have here are three parts to the sentence:

<u>Introductory phrase</u>

> As there is currently no single definition of 'complex needs',

<u>Intermediate phrase</u>

> although the term is frequently used within nursing and learning disability,

<u>Main sentence</u>

> this assignment will use a working definition.

The sentence would make sense without the intermediate or middle phrase, which could almost be an aside or written in brackets. The correct way to punctuate this phrase is to have a comma at either end (not a semicolon), so that, if we lift it out of the sentence altogether, the sentence still makes sense:

> As there is currently no single definition of 'complex needs', this assignment will use a working definition.

We can then reinsert the intermediate phrase, surrounded by commas:

✓ As there is currently no single definition of 'complex needs', although the term is frequently used within nursing and learning disability, this assignment will use a working definition.

An alternative way forward is to **rephrase** the sentence so that it is easier to read, possibly like this:

✓ Although the term is frequently used within nursing and learning disability, there is currently no single definition of 'complex needs', so this assignment will use a working definition.

Challenge 3

How many parts make up this complex sentence below?

(You may like to highlight the different parts in different colours to help.)

Which part is a sentence in its own right?

Which phrase could be in brackets?

> Although ordering and paying for parts is an instant process, delivery in some cases still hasn't met Amazon's current standard, which is why the time scale for this part of the work plan, although arguably the simplest, is set to around three weeks.

Number of parts:

Sentence:

The phrase that could be in brackets:

There are four parts:

1. The introductory phrase -
   Although ordering and paying for parts is an instant process,
2. The main thrust of the sentence and a sentence in its own right -
   delivery in some cases still hasn't met Amazon's current standard,

3. A following phrase (an explanation) -
   which is why the time scale for this part of the work plan is set to around three weeks.
4. An intermediate phrase (the phrase in the middle of the explanation), which acts as an aside or comment and could be in brackets, but is surrounded by commas instead –
   , although arguably the simplest,

   The four parts are separated by commas.

Conclusion

You can have multiple phrases in a sentence, as long as they are punctuated appropriately.

Punctuate these sentences with commas:

The reduction in event-day car parking could encourage event attendees to use public transport which reduces congestion on the roads around Wembley Park as well as reducing emissions of pollutants.
(2 commas to insert)

Secondly the report will examine how the land use has changed by using several colour-coded maps that are dated between 2008 and 2019 detailing what the land use for each plot of land is. (3 commas to insert)

Legal writing often uses very complex sentences, as you can see below. Add commas as appropriate.

Therefore despite the majority view in the case that the courts do possess the institutional ability to declare legislation incompatible with Convention rights the Supreme Court warned against doing so where that would impinge on the role of Parliament. (3 commas)

Whilst the President specifically refused to speculate about what would amount to an "unsatisfactory consideration" the tenor of his judgment against the background of the decisions of those judges who would have granted the declaration strongly suggests that something more than the generality of a Second Reading was contemplated. (3 commas)

✓ **Now compare your answers with those in the 'Corrected versions' on page page 224.**

References as kindly supplied by the student authors

McAllister, M. (2013). Resilience: A personal attribute, social process and key professional resource for the enhancement of the nursing role. PROFESSIONI INFERMIERISTICHE, 66(1) http://www.profinf.net/pro3/index.php/IN/article/view/18

Peters, L., Cant, R., Payne, S., O'Connor, M., McDermott, F., Hood, K., Morphet, J., & Shimoinaba, K. (2013). How death anxiety impacts nurses' caring for patients at the end of life: a review of literature. The open nursing journal, 7, 14–21. https://doi.org/10.2174/1874434601307010014

Parts of Speech

> This section covers the parts of speech mentioned in this book. It sounds old fashioned to be talking about parts of speech, but when we try to clear up the confusion around some homophones, for example, (words that sound the same but are spelt differently), we need to know what a verb is and how it differs from a noun.

The simplest sentence can be just two words long – 'Mike smiled'. It contains a noun (Mike) and a verb (smiled).

A **n**oun is a **n**ame. Both words are four letters long and begin with 'n'.

There are three types of nouns – proper, common, and abstract.

- A proper noun is the name of a person or place, like Mike or England.
- A common noun is the name of 'common' things, like chairs, books, and dogs.
- Abstract nouns are names of things we cannot see, like joy, sadness, and trouble.

* * * * * * * *

Pronoun literally means 'for noun' and a pronoun stands in the place of a noun to avoid excessive repetition. Take the following sentence that repeatedly uses nouns:

> Simon lost Simon's shoes, and Simon was worried when Simon could not find the shoes, but Simon's brother had borrowed the shoes and returned the shoes to Simon that evening.

The sentence sounds much better if we replace some of the nouns with pronouns:

> Simon lost his shoes, and he was worried when he could not find them, but his brother had borrowed them and returned them to him that evening."

Subject pronouns (so called because they begin sentences or are the subject of sentences, as in 'She loves me!') are: *I, you, he, she, it, we* and *they.*

Object pronouns (so called because they are the object of the verb, as in 'She loves me!') are: *me, you, him, her, it, us* and *them.*

****

Verbs are doing words and every sentence must have one.

Examples are:

   I practised, you advised, he examined, she recorded.

****

Two other parts of speech that add depth and detail to sentences are the two 'ads': adjectives and adverbs. Ads on television describe what we really need or must have! Similarly, adjectives and adverbs are describing words.

Adverbs describe verbs and usually (but not always) end in 'ly':

   He laughed happily. She drives slowly, but I drive fast!

Adjectives should really be called 'adnouns' or nouns should be called 'jectives', because adjectives describe nouns!

   A red jumper. A worried look. A huge tree. A delicious meal.

****

Prepositions are small words that often indicate position, such as: on, in, under, over, by, around, behind, beneath, below, near and in front of. The word preposition means 'something that is placed before' and is found before a noun or pronoun, indicating a relation to it, as in: "The book fell off the table" or "The stars disappear from the sky at dawn." Other prepositions include to, for, down, past, through, up, along, across, out of and after.

It used to be said that sentences should never end with a preposition, but it is hard to rephrase "Clear off!". "Off clear!" does not have the same force! Similarly, the famous last words from the introduction to *Star Trek*, "…to boldly go where no man has gone before…" would lose their dramatic appeal if rearranged or rephrased.

However, in academic writing, it is considered good practice to avoid ending sentences with these little words.

****

Conjunctions are little words that join parts of sentences together. The most common are: and, or, but and so.

Other conjunctions include because, although and whether.

Sometimes, conjunctions are combined, as in: not only – but also, either – or, neither – nor, and both – and.

* * * * * * * * *

There is a very helpful poem about the parts of speech that goes like this:

> Every name is called a NOUN, as field and fountain, street and town.
>
> In place of noun, the PRONOUN stands, as he and she can clap their hands.
>
> The ADJECTIVE describes a thing, as magic wand and bridal ring.
>
> The VERB means action, something done – to read, to write, to jump, to run.
>
> How things are done, the ADVERBS tell, as quickly, slowly, badly, well.
>
> The PREPOSITION shows relation, as in the street or at the station.
>
> CONJUNCTIONS join in many ways, sentences, words, or phrase and phrase.
>
> The INTERJECTION cries out, "Hark! I need an exclamation mark!"
>
> Through poetry, we learn how each of these make up THE PARTS OF SPEECH.

Author unknown

Plurals

> Usually, we add an 's' when we make a singular noun become plural. But, of course, the English language is fraught with irregularities and exceptions, and some plural nouns may trip us up! Words that end in 'y' are a good example!

However, there is a nice little rule to help us:

Change the 'y' to an 'i' when you add an ending!

Thus, 'variety' becomes 'varieties', 'agency' becomes 'agencies' and 'economy' becomes 'economies'.

As a matter of interest, the same rule applies to (most!) verbs that end in 'y'. With the verb 'to marry', we write 'they married' and we have a 'marriage' service. However, if we want to add 'ing' at the end of the word, we do not want two 'i's together, so we write 'marrying', not 'marriing'!

Put these single nouns into the plural form, applying the 'y' rule:

facility   quality   agency   fatality   amenity   community

(Answers at the bottom of page 184.)

* * * * * *

Many of my students have needed to learn the 'y' rule, but hopefully plurals were covered and consolidated in your school days. However, if you wish to refresh your memory, you may like to continue reading.

Other letters can change when we make words plural. For example, 'f' changes to 'v', when we make one midwife become plural midwives and one knife becomes plural knives. The same happens with half – halves, life – lives and yourself – yourselves, but there are always exceptions, so it is worth keeping an eye on your spellchecker, as long as you have set it to British English and not American English! If in doubt, ask your best available friend – Google!

* * * * *

Words that end in 'o' usually just add an 's' for the plural form. However, English being the awkward language it is (because it is a pot pourri of numerous languages), there are always exceptions to the rule! Some words ending in 'o' add '<u>es</u>' in the plural form and can be remembered in pairs:

Potato**es** and tomato**es** (edibles)

Tornado**es** and volcano**es** (natural disasters)

Cargo**es** and torpedo**es** (carried on a ship)

Echo**es** and hero**es** (2 syllables)

Domino**es** and mosquito**es** (3 syllables).

They may not crop up in your academic writing, but at least you will know about them if they do!

* * * * * *

The letters 'es' are added to other words too, if they end in what we call 'sibilant' sounds. These are words which sound like a hiss, because the tip of the tongue is brought to the roof of the mouth and air is pushed past the tongue to make a hissing sound: s, x and z, but also ch, tch and sh.

It is very difficult to make the plural form of 'box' become 'boxs' or 'buzz' become 'buzzs' without adding a second syllable. Every syllable must have a vowel, so we add an 'e' as well as the 's', giving us 'box**es**' and 'buzz**es**'. Similarly, if we make a 'glass' become plural by adding an 's', we would have three 's's in a row and the word would still sound as though it had a second syllable. Thus, we write it as 'glass**es**'.

Other examples of plural words ending in 'es' after a sibilant sound are peach**es**, match**es** and wish**es**.

* * * * * *

Three 'oo' words change to 'ee' in the plural:

Tooth – teeth; foot – feet; and goose – geese (but mongoose becomes mongooses!)

* * * * * *

Another oddity! The word 'criteria' often catches people out, because they do not realise it is the plural form of the Latin word, 'criterion'. Remember the difference by thinking of 'one criterion'.

Two other words of Latin origin take the same plural form: one phenomenon becomes plural phenomena and a stratum becomes plural strata.

* * * * * *

Finally, an apparently simple plural often catches students out – women!

Its pronunciation does not help us, as it can sound like 'wimmin'.

If the plural of man is men, then the plural of woman is women. Even if you cannot hear the man and the men in the female version, they are there!

Answers for plural forms of nouns ending in 'y':

    facilities   qualities   agencies   fatalities   amenities   communities

Pruning Excess Words

> A 6000-word essay can sound daunting, so it is sometimes tempting to 'waffle' in order to ensure you meet the word count! Surprisingly, you then find you have exceeded the word count and have to go back and prune the content!

Planning your work in the first place can help: break the assignment down into sections (e.g., Introduction, Point 1, Point 2, Point 3, Discussion, and Conclusion), allocating a word count to each. Bear in mind that 500 words is about 1 page of type. If you allocate 100 words to the Introduction, that is the length of this introduction!

Therefore, keep checking the word count of your different sections. **Be succinct and make every word count**. However, if you are on a creative roll and find you have exceeded your word count, all is not lost! Follow these guidelines to help you remove excess words from your text.

A common example of using excess words is: "By doing something, it…" If you remove the 'by' and 'it', the sentence will be more succinct, should flow better and no comma will be needed. Take this example:

> By hiring George as their wedding planner, it will save the couple time and stress.

This can be rewritten:

> Hiring George as their wedding planner will save the couple time and stress.

✏️ **Take out the two excess words and the comma from these sentences below, inserting capital letters where you need to:**

> By having a wedding planner, it means that they will arrange everything for you, from individual place card settings to all the accommodation for you and your guests.

> By hiring a wedding planner, it should take the stress off the couple to let them enjoy their wedding and the lead up to it.

✏️ **Remove the two different excess words from similar places in these sentences (and commas where appropriate):**

For pregnant women who smoke, they should be offered carbon monoxide (CO) screening at every ante-natal appointment.

Through discussion about the potential harm of smoking in pregnancy, it allows the mother-to-be to make an informed choice regarding support.

Throughout the assignment, it has explored the risks of smoking, and the potential impact it could have on a mother and baby.

With the feasibility study, it will include an itemised budget of all the outgoing costs in relation to the event.

For the wedding reception, this was held at a historic manor on the outskirts of the city.

Seeing Double

> Sometimes, students use twice as many words as they need to, with double nouns, verbs and adjectives when just one would do.

Carers are at a high risk of distress if working with individuals with challenging behavioural issues, and do not have or use effective coping strategies when feeling stressed and frustrated.

This could be rewritten as:

Carers are at a high risk of distress if working with individuals with challenging behavioural issues, and do not <u>use</u> effective coping strategies when feeling <u>frustrated,</u>

There are several permutations, of course, but just one of the words would suffice from each double – and save four words, because you don't need the 'or' or 'and' to link them!

▶ **In the following sentences, there is just one double. They may not have exactly the same meaning but, if you had to prune excess words, highlight which words you would remove.**

Where an employer does not recognize a union, or has fewer than ten employees, information and consultation may take place with the whole workforce.

The proposed name "Naturelle Milk" seems descriptive, except it may be construed as misleading or deceptive by the general public, as a consequence of the product's blend of additives.

The follow-up study findings show that 85% of articles submitted and published contained a sample diversity of less than 7% of the entire world population.

Any agreements or decisions prohibited in accordance with this Article automatically make any contracts unenforceable.

The following sentences contain two sets of doubles.

▶ **Highlight the word you would remove from each double – and any other words you could remove.**

At the end of each sentence, indicate how many words you have saved!

I appreciate and value all the kind words and sentiments I received.

It is also important to make sure* the carer is fully aware of the condition and its progression, so they know and have some understanding of what to expect.

*You could also substitute 'ensure' for 'make sure', saving another word!

Trade secrets require careful and diligent attention to the administration and enforcement of nondisclosure agreements.

Nursing students have numerous fears and anxieties at the beginning of clinical experience, which include making mistakes in practice, the fear of the unknown, and being unsure or not knowing how to do something.

> When pruning your work, look for examples of **'that'** and **'which'** you could delete and replace with the participle ('ing' form) of the verb which follows it.

Take the sentence,

> These often contain clauses **that impose** duties of confidence.

It can be re-written as:

> These often contain clauses, **imposing** duties of confidence.

N.B. Note that a comma replaces the word omitted, in front of the 'ing verb'. You may remember from 'Introductory, Intermediate and Following phrases' that 'ing' verbs suggest a following phrase, which follows a comma.

In the next sentence, 'which' is used twice:

> You are subject to a 'continuing disclosure' obligation, **which** requires you to ensure prompt publicity of any matters **which** are likely to have a substantial effect on the price of the company's shares.

The first '**which**' is followed by a verb (requires) so that '**which**' can be removed and replaced with the participle (requiring). The second use ('**which are**') can also be removed without affecting the sense of the sentence. Thus, the sentence can be pruned of three words like this:

> You are subject to a 'continuing disclosure' obligation, <u>requiring</u> you to ensure prompt publicity of any matters likely to have a substantial effect on the price of the company's shares.

✏️ Remove the 'which' or 'that' from these sentences and replace it with the participle ('ing' form) of the verb that follows, adding a comma if necessary.

Note that the 'e' is dropped from the end of the verb when you add 'ing'.

> My dog, Gus, is wearing a gorgeous bow tie that makes him look absolutely adorable!

> Figure 6 shows the brand's performance against competing brands, which range from the low-end market to the high-end market.

> There is a focus on innovative procedures which provide newly emerging technologies to customers.
>
> I will do this by creating a self-development plan that focuses on myself as a learner, professional, teacher, and member of a team.
>
> I have created a SNOB analysis, which outlines my personal strengths, needs, opportunities and barriers.

Finally, if you need to prune even more words from your work, replace introductory phrases with single words where possible. For example:

- In this way – Therefore or Thus
- In a similar way – Similarly
- An extra idea is that – Also or Additionally
- On the other hand – However
- By contrast – Alternatively
- It is suggested / possible – Arguably
- This is why – Therefore or Thus
- For this reason / As a result – Consequently

Right click on a single word, such as 'similarly', and explore the synonyms. You may get several options and can click on the one you choose to insert into the text. This becomes a treasure hunt and can help expand your vocabulary.

One of my favourite words to use in an assignment is a synonym for 'On the other hand'. Can you guess which one it is? (Answer at the bottom of the next page!)

> **TIP:**
>
> When looking for a synonym, do not put inverted commas around the word, or no synonyms will appear!

✓ Compare your answers with those in the 'Corrected versions' on pages 224-226.

Summary of pruning possibilities:

- Avoid small, unnecessary words, such as 'By …, it' and 'For …, this'.
- Don't use double adjectives, nouns or verbs.
- Take out 'which' or 'that' and replace it with a participle of the verb that follows.
- Check your introductory phrases to see if they can be minimised. Have you used introductory words which are not essential and could be removed?

Look at the next page on 'Rephrasing' to get even more ideas!

My favourite synonym for 'On the other hand' is 'Conversely'.

Rephrasing

Rephrasing is very much part of pruning a word count, but is worth dealing with as a separate skill, as it can be a way to make our work sound more academic.

Effective rephrasing can give your work 'sophisticated gloss' and impress your tutor!

Read the following, uncorrected text:

> The Role of Midwives in Antenatal Education
>
> The National Health Service (NHS) strongly encourages informed choice and consent. Information-sharing helps to facilitate the discussion, supporting parents to make an informed choice about their care (Yuill et al., 2020). The role of the midwife is to support the woman to make an informed choice for her care, parenting styles, empowering women, and promoting a healthy lifestyle during all three stages of pregnancy (Artieta-Pinedo et al., 2017). In 2017, a study released that antenatal education (AE) should be tailored to the needs of the women and their families. This means the role of the midwife is to gain an understanding of the circumstances of the woman and adapt antenatal education to her and not the need of the midwife's workload (Hardie et al., 2014). When supporting a woman to make a choice, you need to be able to listen to the woman and allow for them to feel involved in all elements of the plan of care (Jordan et al., 2014).

Adapted and used with the kind permission of the student author, as indicated in the acknowledgements.

Let's divide this paragraph into 4 sections that could be rephrased:

Section 1

> The National Health Service (NHS) strongly encourages informed choice and consent. Information-sharing helps to facilitate the discussion, supporting parents to make an informed choice about their care (Yuill et al., 2020). **31 words.**

Notes on rephrasing:

- 'Facilitates' means 'helps', so both are not needed in the text.
- 'Regarding' is more specific than 'about'.

- *Two rather cumbersome sentences can be reduced to one flowing sentence.*

Here is a rephrased version, which has cut 9 words in the process:

The National Health Service (NHS) strongly encourages informed choice and consent, facilitating discussion for parents regarding their care (Yuill et al., 2020). **22 words**

✶ ✶ ✶ ✶ ✶ ✶ ✶ ✶ ✶ ✶ ✶ ✶ ✶

Section 2

The role of the midwife is to support the woman to make an informed choice for her care, parenting styles, empowering women and promoting a healthy lifestyle during all three stages of pregnancy (Artieta-Pinedo et al., 2017).
37 words

Notes on rephrasing:

- *It is often possible to remove 'of the' from sentences, by switching the position of the nouns and inserting the possessive apostrophe where appropriate ("midwife's role").*

- *Articles (the/a/an) can be removed to make a general point. For example, "support the (particular) woman to make an informed choice (a specific one)" can be rephrased as "support women (in general) to make informed choices (generally)."*

- *In the original, the second and third line are rather confusing and open to various interpretations. The rephrasing below is just a suggestion. It is not vastly different, and you can see that it is only two words shorter. How would you do it?*

Here is a rephrased version, which has cut just 2 words in the process:

The midwife's role is to support women to make informed choices regarding their care and parenting styles, consequently empowering women and promoting a healthy lifestyle during all three stages of pregnancy (Artieta-Pinedo et al., 2017). **35 words**

✶ ✶ ✶ ✶ ✶ ✶ ✶ ✶ ✶ ✶ ✶ ✶ ✶

Section 3

In 2017, a study released that antenatal education (AE) should be tailored to the needs of the women and their families. This means the role of the midwife is to gain an understanding of the circumstances of the woman and adapt antenatal education to her and not the need of the midwife's workload (Hardie et al., 2014). **57 words**

Notes on rephrasing:

- *Once the acronym AE has been introduced, it is not necessary to use the full title a second time.*
- *'The study' may have been released in 2017, but 'stated' is a better verb to use in the context. 'A 2017 study' sounds neater than 'In 2017, a study…'*
- *'Thus' or 'Therefore' sound better than 'This means'.*

Here is a rephrased version, which has cut 10 words in the process:

A 2017 study stated that antenatal education (AE) should be tailored to the needs of women and their families. Thus, the midwife's role is to gain an understanding of a woman's circumstances, and tailor AE to her and not to the midwife's workload (Hardie et al., 2014). **47 words**

* * * * * * * * * * * * *

Section 4

When supporting a woman to make a choice, you need to be able to listen to the woman and allow for them to feel involved in all elements of the plan of care (Jordan et al., 2014). **37 words**

Notes on rephrasing:

- *Again, we can use plural nouns and omit the indefinite articles (a) and definite articles (the).*
- *It is more academic to write in the third person, objectively referring to 'midwives', rather than say "You need to…".*
- *Don't say "allow for", unless you are explaining, for example, that railway tracks are set with gaps between them to 'allow for' expansion. 'Allow' really means 'permit'. In this context, midwives 'enable' women to be involved; they don't 'permit' involvement!*

This is a rephrased version, which has cut 8 words in the process:

> **When supporting women to make informed choices, midwives must listen to women and enable them to be involved in all elements of their care plan (Jordan et al., 2014).** 29 words

However, one of my students rephrased this even more succinctly, using only 21 words compared to the original 37!

> **When supporting women to make choices, midwives must listen and involve them fully in their care plan (Jordan et al., 2014).** 21 words

References as kindly supplied by the student author:

Artieta-Pinedo, I., Paz-Pascual, C., Grandes, G., and Espinosa, M. (2017). Framework for the establishment of a feasible, tailored and effective perinatal education programme. *BMC Pregnancy and Childbirth.* Vol 17. DOI:10.1186/s12884-017-1234-7

Jordan. R., Engstrom. J., Marfell. J., & Farley. C. (2014). *Prenatal and Postnatal care; A woman-centred approach.* John Wiley & sons.

Hardie. K., Horsburgh. D., and Key. S. (2014). Facilitating AE classes in Scotland. *British Journal of midwifery.* Vol 22. (6). DOI; **10.12968/bjom.2014.22.6.409**

Yuill. C., McCourt. C., Cheyne. H., & Leister. N. (2020). Women's experiences of decision-making and informed choice about pregnancy and birth care: A systematic review and meta-synthesis of qualitative research. *BMC Pregnancy and childbirth.* (20). 343 (2020). DOI **10.1186/s12884-020-03023-6**

* * * * * * * * * * * * *

✏️ **If you would like to hone your rephrasing skills, practise on the following passage:**

(Remember that there is no one correct way of doing this and different people will rephrase it in different ways. Also, you may not necessarily save words when rephrasing; if you are trying to make the meaning clear, you may need to **add** words. Hence, rephrasing is not the same as pruning, although it can help!)

Life in Wembley

Services and facilities available to residents are an integral part of any local community and heavily impact their wellbeing and health. A YouTube video, produced by *The Sports Illustrator* (2020), looks at the Powerleague five-a-side football complex, at risk of closure, beside Wembley Stadium, which offers men's, women's and mixed football leagues. The report interviews Bob, the founder of the Apex Predators football club that plays at the complex. Bob explains the Apex Predators, which has 30 members between ages 16-30, would have to travel 30 minutes to get to another location to train, if the Powerleague closed.

Between 2018 and 2020, the Powerleague complex was replaced by an apartment complex, of apartments costing up to £2,305 pcm (Quintain Living, 2020). These apartments have been completed with their own private facilities, such as gyms and gardens. Now the Powerleague pitches have been lost, this means there are fewer facilities for residents to exercise and socialise within their local community. This could lead to more anti-social behaviour and poor health, having a detrimental effect on the community's wellbeing.

On the other hand, the access to facilities in the local area may have reduced, but the quality of facilities has improved. 56.7% of participants responded they either agreed or strongly agreed that the quality of local facilities and amenities has improved since the opening of the new Wembley Stadium. This shows that, although the number of facilities may be declining, they are improving in quality, which is a huge benefit to the local community. **249 words**

Adapted and used with the kind permission of the student author, as indicated in the acknowledgements.

Try rephrasing this yourself, before comparing your version with the one below:

This is one way to rephrase the passage:

Services and facilities available to residents are an integral part of any local community, heavily impacting their health and wellbeing[1]. A YouTube video, produced by *The Sports Illustrator* (2020), looks at the Powerleague five-a-side football complex, which offers men's, women's and mixed football leagues. The complex is located beside Wembley Stadium and is at risk of closure. The report interviews Bob, the founder of the Apex Predators football club that plays at the complex. Bob explains the Apex Predators, which has 30 members aged from 16–30,[2] would have to travel 30 minutes to get to another location to train, if the Powerleague <u>complex</u>[3] closed.

Between 2018 and 2020, the Powerleague complex was replaced by an apartment complex, each apartment costing up to £2,305 pcm (Quintain Living, 2020). These apartments have been completed with their own private facilities, such as gyms and gardens. Now the Powerleague pitches within the complex have been lost, there are fewer facilities for residents to exercise and socialise within their local community. This could lead to more anti-social behaviour and <u>a decline</u>[4] in health, having a detrimental effect on the community's wellbeing.

The access to facilities in the local area may have reduced, but the quality of facilities has improved. 56.7% of participants <u>in a survey</u>[5] responded they either agreed or strongly agreed that the quality of local facilities and amenities has improved since the opening of the new Wembley Stadium. This shows that the closure of the old Powerleague complex has proven to be a huge benefit to the local community.

TIPS:

Paragraph 1

1. 'Health and wellbeing' trips off the tongue more smoothly than 'wellbeing and health'.

2. We either say 'aged between 16 and 30' or 'aged from 16-(to)30' i.e., 'between…and…' or 'from… to…'

3. Without this clarification, it could suggest that only Wembley has Powerleague pitches, whereas they are found nationally. OR it could suggest that all the Powerleague pitches across the country have been closed.

Paragraph 2

4. 'A decline' suggests the possibility of health issues, whereas 'poor health' sounds as though everybody in the community is guaranteed poor health!

Paragraph 3

5. It needs to be clear what the participants were participating in exactly.

The rephrased version is as follows:

> Services and facilities available to residents are an integral part of any local community, heavily impacting their health and wellbeing. A YouTube video, produced by *The Sports Illustrator* (2020), looks at the Powerleague five-a-side football complex, which offers men's, women's and mixed football leagues. The complex is located beside Wembley Stadium and is at risk of closure. The report interviews Bob, the founder of the Apex Predators football club that plays at the complex. Bob explains the Apex Predators, which has 30 members aged from 16–30, would have to travel 30 minutes to get to another location to train, if the Powerleague complex closed.
>
> Between 2018 and 2020, the Powerleague complex was replaced by an apartment complex, each apartment costing up to £2,305 pcm (Quintain Living, 2020). These apartments have been completed with their own private facilities, such as gyms and gardens. Now the Powerleague pitches within the complex have been lost, there are fewer facilities for residents to exercise and socialise within their local community. This could lead to more anti-social behaviour and a decline in health, having a detrimental effect on the community's wellbeing.
>
> The access to facilities in the local area may have reduced, but the quality of facilities has improved. 56.7% of participants in a survey responded they either agreed or strongly agreed that the quality of local facilities and amenities has improved since the opening of the new Wembley Stadium. This shows that the closure of the old Powerleague complex has proven to be a huge benefit to the local community. **255 words**

Quintain Living. (n.d). *Wembley Park Overview*. QUINTAIN.

https://www.quintain.co.uk/Wembley-park/overview

Conclusion

At 255 words, this rephrased version is slightly longer than the original with 249 words. This does not matter, unless you are exceeding the word count, as long as the rephrasing has clarified the meaning and enhanced the text. For example, here it was important to make it clear that the Powerleague was a complex and that the 56.7% of participants were involved in a survey, which the original text did not. For these reasons, rephrasing is not necessarily the same as pruning, but can often help to reduce a word count!

✏️ **The following paragraph is only 137 words long, but the assignment brief gave a word count of 100 plus or minus 10%. Can you rephrase it to meet the brief?**

> The prescribing team at UNITY (my place of work) consists of a non-medical prescriber (NMP), consultant and community pharmacist. Both the NMP and consultant's role in prescribing is to assess the patient's presenting complaint and decide on the best course of treatment and medication to prescribe (Dhillon and Sodha, 2009). The pharmacist's role is to dispense the medication prescribed by the consultant and NMP to the service user (Tietze, 2012). The boundaries of prescribing for all three professionals are identified by the workplace prescribing policy (GMMH) and their regulatory bodies. The NMP's regulatory body is the NMC, the consultant's is the GMC and the pharmacist's, the General Pharmaceutical Council. An example of a boundary for an NMP is that there should be 'separation of prescribing and administering activities whenever possible', unless there are exceptional circumstances' (NMC, 2006). **137 words**.

One rephrased version that meets the brief at just 104 words long is as follows:

> The prescribing team at work consists of a consultant and a non-medical prescriber (NMP) , whose role is to assess the patient's presenting complaint and prescribe the appropriate treatment (Dhillon and Sodha, 2009), and also a community pharmacist, whose role is to supply the prescribed medication to the patient, who self-administers (Tietze, 2012). The boundaries of prescribing for all three professionals are identified by the workplace's prescribing policy (GMMH), and their regulatory bodies – the NMC (the NMP), the GMC (the consultant) and the GPC (the pharmacist). One boundary for an NMP is there should be 'separation of prescribing and administering activities whenever possible' (NMC, 2006).

References kindly supplied in Harvard style by the student author:

Dhillon, S. and Sodha, M., 2009. *Non-medical prescribing*. 2nd ed. London: Pharmaceutical Press.

Nmc.org.uk. 2006. [online] Available at:

<https://www.nmc.org.uk/globalassets/sitedocuments/standards/nmc-standards-proficiency-nurse-and-midwife-prescribers.pdf>

[Accessed 6 February 2021].

Tietze, K., 2012. *Clinical skills for pharmacists*. St. Louis, Mo.: Elsevier Mosby.

'Th' and 'wh' Words

> 'Th' words often begin sentences.
>
> 'Th' words sound emphatic and are used to begin sentences.

Look at the examples of 'th' words beginning sentences that are highlighted yellow in the following passage. The words highlighted orange begin sentences that have been attached to the previous sentence with a link word or phrase.

The opening ceremony for an event will normally differ from the rest of the event, as they usually have an element of entertainment, whether that be live music, dancers or performers. There will still be an agenda for the opening ceremony and there will often be guest speakers, so the event is mixed. Overall,* the agenda for the opening ceremony will be light-hearted and fun, with the focus on the attendees enjoying themselves. This can differ from the rest of an event if its main focus is to concentrate on business or the serious side of the event.

*Here the sentence begins with a 'th' word AFTER the introductory word.

Of course, not all sentences begin with 'th' words!

1. How many sentences are there in the passage below? (Tip: Highlight each full stop to help you.)
2. How many of these sentences **begin** with a 'th' word?

The NICE guidelines suggest midwives should continue to ask pregnant women about their smoking status and praise or advise where necessary (NICE, 2018). These guidelines help support the behaviour change theory of the COM-B Model. The COM-B Model analyses what an individual requires to be able to make changes to their life, examining the behaviours and resources that the individual has. A pregnant woman needs to have the psychological and physical capability to perform the change (West & Brown, 2013). This includes skills and tools to be able to stop smoking. Not all women need to have Nicotine replacement therapy to help them, but they need to have the knowledge how to stop. This is where the referral from the midwife to the NHS Stop Smoking Service can help (NHS, 2020).

✏️ **Look for the new sentences here that begin with a 'th' word and insert full stops and capital letters, as appropriate. Feel free to add commas as well!**

As well as capability the woman needs to have the social and physical opportunity, this includes giving the woman time to make the change as smoking is an addiction.

However, to make a change, the woman needs to have the motivation to do this, this is where information shared between the woman and the midwife can potentially help the woman.

I would often liaise with the social worker and other multidisciplinary teams to ensure that service users' issues were dealt with and resolved, therefore having a satisfactory outcome, this inspired me to become a social worker.

✏️ **Insert the missing commas and full stops in this passage:**

This activity promotes creativity for children, through this activity children express new ideas and use resources to represent their ideas. Creativity helps children develop problem-solving abilities and think of solutions using imagination and application of knowledge, therefore this activity promotes an outcome of value and worth through creativity because the children accomplish a creative task the work is praised and they feel appreciated thus the children were able to have their self-esteem and confidence boosted.

✓ Now compare your answers with those in the 'Corrected versions' on pages 226 and 227.

Sometimes you can change 'this' to 'which' and use a comma instead of a full stop before it. Consider this sentence:

Maslow (1943) presented a different approach to the humanistic psychology, this is known as Maslow's Hierarchy of Needs.

It can either be written as, "Maslow (1943) presented a different approach to the humanistic psychology. This is known as Maslow's Hierarchy of Needs."

OR it could be written as, "Maslow (1943) presented a different approach to the humanistic psychology, which is known as Maslow's Hierarchy of Needs."

> 'Wh' words are **link** words and often follow commas.

Consider these original sentences:

> "The NHS wants to increase staffing levels. Which could have the potential to help with community hubs."

This can EITHER be written, "The NHS wants to increase staffing levels, which could have the potential to help with community hubs."

OR, "The NHS wants to increase staffing levels. This could have the potential to help with community hubs."

OR (using a colon between the two, to introduce the explanatory sentence which follows, for sophisticated gloss to impress your tutor again!), "The NHS wants to increase staffing levels:* this could have the potential to help with community hubs."

*The colon almost replaces the word 'because' to link the two sentences. See the teaching pages on 'Colons, Semicolons, Dots and Dashes' (starting on page 128) for further explanation.

Exception to the Rule:

It is important to check whether the 'which' is going on to give more detail or an explanation, and whether the sentence could have ended where you put the comma.

For example:

> I believe it is important to identify in advance any other events which may compete with the event you are in the process of organising.

Firstly, the sentence would not really make sense in the context if there was a full stop after 'events'. Secondly, the 'which' is not adding a reason or extra detail. The object of the 'identification' is "events which may compete…" In such a case, it is perfectly acceptable grammatically not to use a comma before the 'which'. However, if you prefer to be consistent with your punctuation, substitute 'that' for 'which' and omit the comma, because a comma is not used before 'that':

> I believe it is important to identify in advance any other events **that** may compete with the event you are in the process of organising.

Advanced Grammar:

Can you spot what is grammatically wrong with the following sentence?

> The new development is reducing the public space which the local community has access to.

Does it need a comma before the 'which'?

Answer: No, because the object of the sentence is "the public space which (or that) the local community…"

The actual problem is that the sentence ends with 'to', which is a preposition and not supposed to end a sentence. We can, however, change the position of 'to' in the sentence and **follow it with 'which'**, like this:

> The new development is reducing the public space to which the local community has access.

Other prepositions are similarly combined with 'which' to avoid the same grammatical problem. For example, instead of writing,

> The foundations were ready to build the house on,

we can add 'which' to the preposition 'on' and write,

> The foundations were ready **on which** to build the house.

Similarly, in the sentence,

> It was not clear which child the present was intended for,

we can add 'which' to the preposition 'for' and write,

> It was not clear **for which** child the present was intended.

If the word 'who' replaces 'which child', we use 'whom' instead of 'which'. Therefore, with the sentence,

> It was not clear who the present was intended for,

we can add 'whom' to the preposition 'for' and write,

> It was not clear **for whom** the present was intended.

'Wh' words LINK!

They do not start sentences unless they are part of an introductory phrase or asking a question.

Consider these examples:

> *Titus Groan*, by Mervyn Peake (1946), is a fantasy set in the fictional castle of Gormenghast, **where** traditions are strictly followed and lifepaths predetermined at birth.

> In the story, Norse elements link the main female character with her aunts, **who** are forgotten members of the castle.

> Let me take you to a mythical land shrouded in the mists of time, **when** unicorns roamed free, and mermaids sang.

While/Whilst

It is fine to use 'whilst' as an alternative to 'while', as long as you include the 'l' and don't end up with 'whist'!

Example 1

The female penguin looks after the eggs **while** the male hunts for food.

This could have been two short, balanced sentences, perhaps separated by a semicolon:

The female penguin looks after the eggs**;** the male hunts for food.

Using 'while' as a link word helps the sentences flow, and also conveys the sense of the male and female doing separate activities at the same time.

When 'while' or 'whilst' means 'at the same time', <u>no</u> comma is used before it.

Example 2

The image of Laurie represents her free and confident personality **whilst** it is still delicate and feminine.

Again, this could be two short, balanced sentences:

The image of Laurie represents her free and confident personality**. It** is still delicate and feminine.

However, this sounds choppy and there is no sense of the link between the sentences. You could use 'but' to join the sentences, although 'whilst' conveys the idea that:

The image of Laurie represents her free and confident personality **whilst** (at the same time) it is still delicate and feminine.

'Whilst' does not have to link sentences but can simply link parts of a sentence. The author of this sentence actually wrote:

The image of Laurie represents her free and confident personality **whilst still being** delicate and feminine.

This sounds gentler than using the rather clunky 'it is still…' I try to avoid using 'it' if I can. Using the word 'being' sounds more melodious and flowing.

If you use 'while' or 'whilst' to mean 'whereas' or 'although', it is used as a comparison, so put a comma before it. For example:

The Beatles are as popular as ever, while the Monkees have been largely forgotten.

Whereas

Consider this example:

> In a vast venue, mobile phones rely on receiving the correct signal and may lose signal, whereas internal telephone lines will work regardless.

This could again be two sentences:

> In a vast venue, mobile phones rely on receiving the correct signal and may lose signal. Internal telephone lines will work regardless.

But you are **comparing** two kinds of phone, so it makes sense to keep them in the same sentence and link them with 'whereas'.

> **'Whereas' is used to compare one idea against another and link them in the same sentence.**

➤ **Put commas in front of the 'wh' words where appropriate in the sentences below.**

Ensure the 'wh' word does **not** begin a sentence!

> I chose this because of the lapels which are not featured on other patterns I found.

> A smaller part would be more appealing to the actor who would then not have to memorise so many lines.

> Introductory words include useful link words, like 'Therefore', 'Consequently', 'However' and 'Furthermore' which are always followed by a comma to separate them from the rest of the sentence.

> Two of the three participants were able to form a strong connection to the deaf community and the use of sign language whereas one participant struggled to identify with the deaf community and sign language, due to his late diagnosis.

> The monochrome image used for Robert, with intertwined shapes running through it, represents his powerful and stern presence whilst also representing that there is more going on in his life than first thought.

The linear, harsh lines of the geometric shapes represent the intimidating nature of the powerful, older characters. Whilst the flowing, natural shapes and lines represent the feelings of romance, youthfulness and fun, encapsulating the socialite characters.

You can also have introductory phrases which usually set the scene or give a detail. They are also separated from the rest of the sentence by a comma.

In the 1990 film version of *The Handmaid's Tale*, the costumes have changed from those described in the book, with the handmaids not being as concealed as in the novel where even their faces are hidden by a winged habit.

The difference in size between the two flats could be down to many reasons: it could be because the first flat was constructed at a time when there was a large deficit in housing after the First World War whereas the second flat was not.

After the four-week trial period is over, the researcher can suggest a time to meet up when the participant can share with him the impact of the intervention.

Findings suggest that it is appearance training in conversations with friends that leads to changes in body dissatisfaction in girls. Whereas for the boys, it was the internalization of body ideal that led to changes in body dissatisfaction (Carlson Jones, 2004).

The conduct of the President left many people feeling that the United States had reverted back to an old way of thinking where women were objectified for sex appeal and were not equal to their male counterparts. This has a correlation with *The Handmaid's Tale* when society has advanced but then regresses back to an older philosophy. (2 to find)

✓ **Compare your answers with those in the 'Corrected versions' on pages 227-229.**

Whether

This is not strictly a link word, but often sounds better than 'if'.

Consider this example:

> This method would enable nurses to monitor if the intervention was valuable or not.

> This method would enable nurses to monitor whether the intervention was valuable or not.

Which do you prefer?

References in order of appearance:

NICE. (2018). *Stop smoking interventions and services.* Retrieved from: https://www.nice.org.uk/guidance/ng92#engaging-with-people-who-smoke

West, R. & Brown, J. (2013). **Theory of Addiction.** *John Wiley & Sons.*

NHS, (2020). *Local stop smoking services.* Retrieved from: https://www.nhs.uk/smokefree/help-and-advice/local-support-services-helplines

Peake, M. (1946). *Titus Groan.* Eyre & Spottiswoode Ltd.

Maslow, A.H. (1943). A Theory of Human Motivation. *Psychological Review, 50,* 370–396

Carlson Jones, D. (2004). Body Image Among Adolescent Girls and Boys: A Longitudinal Study. Developmental Psychology, 40(5), 823–835. https://doi.org/10.1037/0012-1649.40.5.823

CORRECTED VERSIONS

A and An

The correct article has been inserted in the following sentences:

> Actin is specifically folded so it has to stabilise areas with <u>an</u> adenosine nuclide between them.

> DNA has <u>a</u> double helix structure to keep it stable.

> The scientist had <u>an</u> established formula.

> Registered nurses are also looked at as nursing educators, due to the fact that you have achieved <u>a</u> high-level master's nursing degree.

As and Has

'Has' is inserted in the correct place in these sentences:

> This disciplinary panel discussed what the student <u>has</u> done to improve his attendance so far.

> Most residents agreed that the provision of public transport <u>has</u> improved in recent years.

> President Biden <u>has</u> replaced Donald Trump as President of the USA.

> As there <u>has</u> been a case of Covid 19 among the restaurant staff, the meal <u>has</u> been cancelled. (2 replaced)

Agreement of Verbs

- The legato notes in the bass <u>make</u> the listener feel very relaxed.
- Writing development plans <u>enables</u> the individual to develop their learning skills.
- Membership <u>declines</u> because of the ageing membership profile.
- I have gained an understanding of some of the daily responsibilities of a social worker and the issues families <u>experience</u>.

- The main argument addressed in the debate is that adult care needs are often multiple and intersect with other issues.

- Peters et al. (2013) claim younger nurses are reported to have a stronger fear of death, possibly because they may not be experienced or well skilled in dealing with the impact on their emotions.

- Other researchers that have conducted some cross-cultural research are Bleidorn et al. (2013).

- We must ensure the nitrogen base of the DNA cell is not damaged.

- There is now a broader set of child wellbeing outcomes to apply to each case.

- I care about others, I have compassion and am always willing to put others' needs before mine.

- There are still numerous barriers we could have to face.

- The provision of essential information and resources is vital for service users' wellbeing.

- Before I was diagnosed with dyslexia, I just thought I wasn't as bright as other students were.

- The course of antibiotics has been completed.

- The competition for leisure time has caused relative market growth to slow.

- Wembley Park is increasingly trying to attract visitors into the area through various entertainment and hospitality outlets that have been opened.

- The questionnaire results confirm that most residents agree that public transport links have improved since the construction of Wembley Stadium.

- The documentary showed what goes into the making of images and how the different decisions that are made during the creative process have a big impact on the viewer's experience.

- Other parameters used in the article are: the employment the events held at the stadium have provided, money generated through events and whether the area has retained that money.

- The government wants to reduce maternal and neonatal mortality by 2025.

- The World Health Organisation (WHO) <u>has</u> termed Covid 19 a pandemic.
- The United Nations (UN) <u>is</u> made up of 193 member states.
- The NHS <u>has</u> published a new plan called 'NHS Long Term'.
- The Royal College of Midwives (RCM) <u>has</u> approved the plan for community hubs.
- The Parish Council <u>has</u> twelve members.
- The NHS <u>is</u> working with universities around the country to expand the number of applicants for nursing courses.
- The cohort <u>was</u> clearly in peak physical condition.
- The Higher Education Statistics Agency (HESA) <u>collects</u> individual university statistics on behalf of the UK government to inform the public of a university's performance.

Challenge 1 – Corrections Underlined

A Critical Appraisal Skills Programme (CASP) <u>was</u> used to assess the quality of the individual articles selected. This systematic process incorporates trustworthiness, ensuring relevance, and <u>confirms</u> the results of each individual article (Critical Appraisal Skills Programme, 2018). The allocated studies for the review <u>were</u> cohort studies (n=3) and RCTs (n=2). Two different CASP checklist tools were used, based on the specific design. There <u>are</u> three sections to the CASP tool, which aims to analyse the validity of the articles. A quality score <u>was</u> used, based on these three sections and questions answering Yes, No or Unclear. Those answering No or Unclear were used to assess the reasoning for these answers. A quality assessment table <u>was</u> constructed, based on the CASP forms, which were then rated as either high, medium and low quality. (6 errors)

Thematic analysis is the discovery of patterns within content, in which themes are developed and analysed as a whole and <u>bring</u> together data to synthesise. The variable outcomes within the studies <u>are</u> extracted and reported as themes within this literature review, in a similar way that conceptual themes are derived from qualitative data. Experts in the field <u>state</u> that thematic analysis <u>lacks</u> transparency, due to when and how the themes are allocated and identified. (4)

A Prisma Flow diagram (Fig. 1) <u>was</u> then constructed as a visual presentation of the search strategy. PRISMA stands for: Preferred

Reporting Items for Systematic Reviews and Meta-Analysis and <u>takes</u> into consideration a four-phase flow diagram process that <u>ensures</u> transparency. However, it is displayed in a simplistic manner which <u>does</u> not include the detail of how the systematic review or meta-analysis is conducted. (4)

Although

Commas inserted after, around or before the 'although phrases' below:

> Although it is no longer an offence to take one's own life, it remains an offence to assist a suicide.

> The motives behind drinking alcohol are multifactorial and, although alcohol may provide a short-term solution, it can contribute to disease and premature death long term.

> Although most of the students who visited the health promotion stand agreed that the promotion of alcohol awareness was good, they were limited to completing a questionnaire.

> Steve Reich is arguably one of the most influential composers of the twentieth century, although his own work was influenced by Bartok and other well-known composers.

> In 2005, it was found that almost a third of mothers in England smoked in the last 12 months before pregnancy (National Institute for Health and Care Excellence [NICE], 2010), although smoking among women who are pregnant has fallen in recent years.

Apostrophes – Inserted

> That dog's lead has broken.
>
> The three dogs' owners were shouting at them.
>
> The ginger cat's milk had spilt everywhere.
>
> York College's principal is retiring.
>
> Not all the actors' scripts were delivered to them on time.
>
> The UK government's plan backfired!

The planets' orbits are almost circular whereas a comet's orbit is elliptical. (2 to find)

In the orchestra, all the musicians' attention was focused on the conductor's baton. (2 to find)

The men's team was very successful.

The sheep's trough was full of water.

The children's playground was colourful and inviting.

Princess Diana was known as 'the People's Princess'.

This finding suggests that frequent intervention could have an impact in increasing participants' perceived severity of their condition and subsequent behaviour change.

Multi-agency working is vital to effective safeguarding and child protection. The team is formed around each individual service user's concerns.

The interviews will be analysed to collect data for both focus groups' discussions.

At the university's health centre, the podiatrist addressed Joe's feet's bunions.

The dentist's opinion was that Tina's teeth's enamel had worn away.

Due to Harry's mother's strong love shielding Harry, Voldemort's spell rebounded on him.

Apostrophes inserted in contracted forms

I have **I've**	are not **aren't**	you are **you're**
would not **wouldn't**	we had **we'd**	there would **there'd**
is not **isn't**	you have **you've**	could not **couldn't**
I will **I'll**	it is **it's**	should have **should've**
there will **there'll**	did not **didn't**	*shall not **shan't**

*Note that "shall not" is contracted unusually, probably because over the years "shalln't" became further contracted to "shan't".

Contractions restored to their full form, without an apostrophe:

I'd **I had/would**	she's **she is**	wasn't **was not**
they'd **they had/would**	we've **we have**	shouldn't **should not**

it'd it had/would	can't cannot	we're we are
you'd you had/would	they'll they will	would've would have
there's there is	don't do not	*won't will not

*The history of the contraction *won't* is very interesting. Apparently, in Old English there were two forms of the verb *willan*, meaning to wish or will: *wil* for the present tense and *wold* for the past tense. Over time, pronunciation changed and *wil not* became *woll not*. This was contracted to *wonnot*, which was further contracted to *won't*.

Been or Being – Inserted

I have coloured black the 'h' word accompanying a 'been' to consolidate the point.

I was about to face my toughest challenge yet – an undergraduate degree. It wasn't going to be easy, especially not being able to read all that well.

There have been some amazing shooting stars in the skies recently.

A fine for not adhering to social distancing rules has been introduced.

Having been evicted by her landlord, the student had to find new accommodation.

I am being very lazy today!

Being a professional musician has been my ambition since childhood.

In each sentence below, 'have' has replaced the incorrect 'of' where appropriate:

It would have been more effective to have an interactive activity for students to measure what they thought a unit of alcohol was; they could have used water in place of the alcohol.

The footballers should have known better than to go out drinking the night before the match.

I would have thought the government could have cut inflation by now.

The University should have ensured Freshers' Week went ahead with online activities.

Lectures should not have been cancelled. Pre-recorded lectures could have been shown online instead.

The student's marks must not have been added up correctly. She could have failed had her tutor not realised the grade was inaccurate.

Colons and Semicolons – Inserted

Colons inserted in these sentences:

I am proactive in my personal development: my most recent qualification was achieved through the Northern Council for Further Education (NCFE). (E)

Some individuals have serious and/or multiple needs, which can affect all areas of their lives: social, psychological, emotional, physical, intellectual, and spiritual. (L)

In the fashion industry, there are two distinctive paths for sustainability in material reuse: recycle and upcycle. (L)

Marilyn Monroe was attributed with saying the following: "Give a girl the right shoes, and she can conquer the world." (Q)

The team working in partnership is essential to support the critical principle of information-sharing, which should be: proportionate, necessary, relevant, accurate, timely, and secure. (L)

Each jacket I upcycled was a different size, so the panels in the backs were different: some of the jackets had thin panels in the back and others had wide. (E)

Statements divided with a semicolon:

Cut the passing thread so that two pieces are laid over the felt; each end should have a large tail.

Use waxed thread and sew the two passing threads down; each stitch should be around 4 mm apart.

Corporate events are run by organisations; they can be for a variety of audiences.

Security is especially important when you are running events where children are in attendance; you may need an added form of security protection if there are celebrities, politicians, or anyone in the public eye at the event.

Integrated working is to provide unified support to service users with multiple and complex needs; it is used as a preventative and early intervention method, as it reduces risk factors that contribute to a poor outcome for children and young people.

Semicolons and a colon inserted into each sentence below, replacing commas where necessary:

I was provided with training in four areas: Introduction to care; moving and handling; first aid; and medication.

Some individuals have serious and/or multiple needs that can affect all areas of their lives: social, psychological, emotional, physical, intellectual, and spiritual; they challenge us as caregivers to provide responsive solutions.

With the planning for any event, the fundamentals are very similar: find out the purpose of the event and plan the event accordingly; choose an appropriate venue; produce a relevant theme; invite the target audience; have a project plan and itinerary; and keep within budget.

The areas I feel I could improve whilst on placement are: firstly, setting small, manageable, and achievable goals to improve my learning in a specific timeframe; secondly, prioritise tasks through the day; and thirdly, achieve a good work-life balance.

The wedding planner's duties will include: managing the guest logistics; working with the venue/s; managing external staff, as well as internal staff; meet any external suppliers and manage their deliveries; and simply ensure that the wedding goes exactly to plan.

Complex Example Punctuated:

The author attempted to contact eight resident associations from areas in Brent, because residents' associations are typically heavily involved in local issues, and five Wembley-based Facebook groups: friends of Eton Grove Park; Quintain Living Wembley Residents Group; What's happening on Preston Road, Wembley Park; 'All things in Wembley, local info, selling, services, and more…'; and 'You know you come from Wembley if…'.

Revision Challenge:

One colon and three semicolons have been inserted in this passage, so that it is a list of factors introduced by a colon, with each of the three factors separated by a semicolon, and the last two factors linked with 'and'.

When choosing a conference venue, there are three important factors that need to be taken into consideration: the venue must meet the needs of the conference, including providing the presenters with the correct equipment, and the delegates with suitable catering, rooms, seating, lighting, materials etc.; the venue must be of the right capacity for the event and contain the correct number of break-out rooms, which will need to be set up according to the client's preferred layout; and the location of the venue is critical, as it will need to have good transport links to open the event up to delegates from across the country.

Commas – Inserted

Steph stated that she is working towards a community detox with her keyworker, and her keyworker has advised she will be prescribed Thiamine Hydrochloride.

To reflect his status, the landowner's clothes are made from good quality fabrics, such as his waxed cotton dungarees, lined with sheepskin, and his waterproof animal hide coat.

Vygotsky's (1978) theory of child development can be used to understand the psychological components influencing the child-teacher relationship, and how this relationship can affect the development of the child.

The author defines the evidence-based approach to improve decision-making, and the use of evidence is more effective than subjective hunches.

The Barça Innovation Hub has a 'Robot Pol'. This enabled children to visit Camp Nou, using a remote-controlled robot, and a 16-year-old was also visited by one of the players.

The article utilized the following parameters to analyse whether an area is at risk of or undergoing gentrification: household income, housing prices, % of renters, % of non-white, % of higher education, and housing affordability.

A survey demonstrated that, of the 56 maternity units within the UK that responded, 73% offered colostrum harvesting advice to diabetic women, 25% offered advice to women who had risk factors, while 19% offered advice to all women (Pathak, 2017).

First and Third Person – Amended

This reflection will use Rolfe's structure rather than Gibbs' reflective cycle.

Findings suggest that frequent text intervention could have an impact in increasing participants' perceived severity of their condition.

The interviews will be analysed to collect data for both focus groups.

An article read by the researcher analyses the 'still image' and opens up the mind to how there are many different variables that go into an image.

The variables are vast, so a few will be named and discussed individually to explain how they can change the viewer's perspective of the image.

Hyphens – Inserted

A hyphen is inserted where one is needed in these sentences. Remember that if the noun comes **before** the describing words, **no** hyphen is needed!

Midwifery is a research-informed profession.

Evidence-based practice is embraced internationally as the ideal approach to improving healthcare outcomes.

The study used in-depth interviews and a qualitative analysis method to determine themes.

The government's aim is to become a smoke-free society within the next five years.

Occasionally, I use rather long-winded sentences, so I was encouraged to condense them.

Stitching by hand was considerably more time consuming but was more effective. (No hyphen is needed, because the noun precedes the compound adjective.)

According to woman-centred care, the plan given to a woman is tailored to her needs.

A long-term study was recommended, using historical records.

These select individuals have openly shared that they like to invest their money in quality-driven, innovative designs.

> The brand plans to launch their first pop-up store in London within one year of launching.
>
> The brand also aims to secure UK concessions in high-end department stores, as mentioned in the brand's objectives.
>
> The brand's consumers always have the assurance that they will be investing in products which are fashionable and on trend. (No hyphen is needed in 'on trend' because the noun precedes the compound adjective.)

More than one hyphen is inserted in these sentences

> One-to-one, semi-structured interviews will be used to obtain rich data.
>
> Diet education will inform Ben about food alternatives he can eat that won't increase his blood glucose levels, such as sugar-free and low-sugar alternatives.
>
> It is important to have a pre-event briefing with all the participants, as it ensures a smooth-running and well-organised event.
>
> The teams and organisations can promote anti-oppressive and anti-discriminatory practices, by allowing individuals to take control of their affairs, support organisations, and employ a strengths-based approach that allows people to manage their data.
>
> With the expansion of the Metropolitan Railway in 1863, people were able to trade the rat-ridden, disease-infested streets of central London for healthy countryside.
>
> From this, it can be inferred that whilst cross-cultural research is being conducted, there is yet to be a time-efficient, cost-effective way of conducting such research.
>
> The book is set in a post-apocalyptic future, with sub-zero temperatures in a life-threatening environment.
>
> Another important change in land use is the stark increase of high-rise housing, due to a regeneration plan to build over 6,000 homes, as part of what aims to be the largest single-site, purpose-built, build-to-rent development anywhere in the UK.
>
> The company is positioned at the low end of the luxury market. Figure 6 shows the company against key, competing brands, ranging from the low-end market to the high-end market.

Note here that 'the <u>low end</u> of the market' is not hyphenated, as the adjective used to describe 'the end' is just one word – 'low'. However, when you describe the market as being 'low end', you use two words to make one adjective, so it needs the hyphen!

Hyphens inserted where appropriate in these sentences:

> The ring had a mother-of-pearl stone.
>
> My dad built a lean-to on the side of the house.
>
> The dancer had dramatic make-up.
>
> My brother left his comrades-in-arms back in Iraq.
>
> Pre-war council houses are currently being refurbished.
>
> The build-up to the release of the last Harry Potter film was captivating.
>
> Andrew Lloyd-Webber has written so many beautiful musicals.
>
> Many of the steel-producing plants in Sheffield closed in the 1970s.
>
> Three-times Wimbledon champion, Boris Becker, commentated on the match.
>
> A well-thought-out plan makes writing a cohesive essay much easier.
>
> Tracy-Ann Oberman starred in the sitcom, *Friday Night Dinner*, for ten years.
>
> I was glad of my third-party insurance after I bumped into another car.
>
> 'Seventy-six Trombones' is the signature song in the musical, *The Music Man*.
>
> A one-day-old baby was found on the steps of the Public Library.
>
> Midwives carry out post-natal checks on all new mums.
>
> The poet, Cecil Day-Lewis, also wrote mystery stories under the pseudonym, Nicholas Blake.
>
> A red-haired, ten-year-old girl is required for the main role in *Annie*.
>
> The anti-abortion campaigners filmed a pro-life documentary.

Introductory, Intermediate and Following Phrases – Corrected

Commas have been inserted after the introductory words and phrases in each sentence below:

> According to experts, the life cycle of Magellanic penguins follows a certain pattern. In September, the penguins return to their nests. In October, the female lays two eggs. In November, the eggs are incubated for 40 days. Initially, the female looks after the eggs while the male hunts for food. When hatched in December or January, the parents take it in turns to look after the young. During this time, the other parent searches for food in the sea (blogpatagonia.australis.com, 2017).

> Early on, I was nominated as the team leader who would coordinate the discussions, set up meetings on Teams, and bring the slides together to form the presentation. At the start, I was worried about taking on the leadership role, but was happy to do so, as I was able to make sure everyone took part. After the presentation, I received positive feedback from the group about my leadership skills. However, I found that I try to make everyone happy to avoid conflict. Within social work, there will be conflict and challenge at times, when I will need to become assertive.

Commas have been inserted between the main sentence and the following phrase in the following sentences:

> Figure 6 shows the brand's performance against competing brands, ranging from the low-end market to the high-end market.

> There is a focus on innovative procedures, providing newly emerging technologies to customers.

> I will create a self-development plan, focusing on myself as a learner, professional, teacher, and member of a team.

> I have created a SNOB analysis, outlining my personal strengths, needs, opportunities and barriers.

> Students are bound to have anxieties at the beginning of their university experience, including finding their way around the campus, managing coursework, and achieving a good work-life balance.

A comma has been inserted before the start of the following phrase, and the word which follows the comma highlighted:

The brand uses recognisable, brown, recycled packaging, which is seen throughout the brand's e-commerce packaging, in-store packaging, swing tags and branding.

Peters et al. (2013) claim younger nurses are reported to consistently have a stronger fear of death, because they may not be experienced or well skilled in dealing with the emotional side of the experience.

The reason I performed this section in multiple steps was so that I could understand and see what else resided within each directory, as well as show other steps which have been performed.

Different words used to introduce the following phrase in the sentences below:

McAllister (2013) states resilience strategies are integral to nursing practice, due to assisting patients and families to cope with many types of adversity.

Five different locations will be compared to show the reader the changes over time, with secondary research used to give more detail about the changes.

The study found over 20% of participants experienced the floor effect, so there is very little variance in the results.

Words that introduced the following phrase in the sentences above:

which, because, as (well as), due (to), with, & so.

Commas have been placed around the intermediate words and phrases in the sentences below:

The main role of the social worker, however, is to care for people.

It is important, therefore, to keep an eye on your word count for an essay, so that you do not have to go back and prune it!

Semicolons have a different function, incidentally, from colons and dashes.

The easiest way to proofread your work is to read it aloud, as though to a packed lecture room, and punctuate your pauses for breath.

Firstly, using an article from the Sports Illustrator, a specific case study will be analysed.

The girl dashed out of the building and, running hurriedly to her car, slipped on some ice.

> Start in the middle and, as the stitches move outwards, cut away the centre bottom string.

> The motives behind drinking alcohol are multifactorial and, although alcohol may provide a short-term solution, it can contribute to disease and premature death in the long term.

Punctuated Sentences:

> The reduction in event-day car parking could encourage event attendees to use public transport, which reduces congestion on the roads around Wembley Park, as well as reducing emissions of pollutants.

> Secondly, the report will examine how the land use has changed, by using several colour-coded maps that are dated between 2008 and 2019, detailing what the land use for each plot of land is.

Legal writing often uses very complex sentences, as you can see below. Do you agree with the punctuation suggested?

> Therefore, despite the majority view in the case that the courts do possess the institutional ability to declare legislation incompatible with Convention rights, the Supreme Court warned against doing so, where that would impinge on the role of Parliament.

> Whilst the President specifically refused to speculate about what would amount to an "unsatisfactory consideration", the tenor of his judgment, against the background of the decisions of those judges who would have granted the declaration, strongly suggests that something more than the generality of a Second Reading was contemplated.

Excess Words Pruned

Two excess words and the comma have been removed from these sentences below, with capital letters inserted where needed:

> Having a wedding planner means that they will arrange everything for you, from individual place card settings to all the accommodation for you and your guests.

> Hiring a wedding planner should take the stress off the couple to let them enjoy their wedding and the lead up to it.

Two different excess words have been removed from similar places in these sentences (and commas where appropriate):

> Pregnant women who smoke should be offered carbon monoxide (CO) screening at every ante-natal appointment.

> Discussion about the potential harm of smoking in pregnancy allows the mother-to-be to make an informed choice regarding support.

> The assignment has explored the risks of smoking, and the potential impact it could have on a mother and baby.

> The feasibility study will include an itemised budget of all the outgoing costs in relation to the event.

> The wedding reception was held at a historic manor on the outskirts of the city.

Words that could be removed from each double have been ==highlighted==.

I have highlighted the word (and link word) I would remove, but you could choose the other word in the double to remove, if you think it makes more sense that way.

> Where an employer does not recognize a union, or has fewer than ten employees, ==information and== consultation may take place with the whole workforce.

> The proposed name "Naturelle Milk" seems descriptive, except it may be construed as misleading ==or deceptive== by the general public as a consequence of the product's blend of additives.

> The follow-up study findings show that 85% of articles ==submitted and== published contained a sample diversity of less than 7% of the entire world population.

> Any agreements ==or decisions== prohibited in accordance with this Article automatically make any contracts unenforceable.

For the next four practice sentences, words you could remove from each double are highlighted ==yellow==. Any other words you could remove are highlighted ==green==.

I have indicated how many words could be saved this way, at the end of each sentence.

> I appreciate ==and value== ==all== the kind words ==and sentiments== I received. 5

It is also important to make ensure the carer is fully aware of the condition and its progression, so they know and have some understanding of what to expect. 10

Trade secrets require careful and diligent attention to the administration and enforcement of nondisclosure agreements. 4

Nursing students have numerous fears and anxieties at the beginning of clinical experience, which include making mistakes in practice, the fear of the unknown, and being unsure or not knowing how to do something. 5

'That' or 'which' removed from these sentences, with an 'ing' verb added after a comma:

Note that the 'e' is dropped from the end of the verb when you add 'ing'.

My dog, Gus, is wearing a gorgeous bow tie, making him look absolutely adorable!

Figure 6 shows the brand's performance against competing brands, ranging from the low-end market to the high-end market.

There is a focus on innovative procedures, providing newly emerging technologies to customers.

I will do this by creating a self-development plan, focusing on myself as a learner, professional, teacher, and member of a team.

I have created a SNOB analysis, outlining my personal strengths, needs, opportunities and barriers.

'Th' and 'wh' Words

'Th' words often begin sentences

The NICE guidelines suggest midwives should continue to ask pregnant women about their smoking status and praise or advise where necessary (NICE, 2018). These guidelines help support the behaviour change theory of the COM-B Model. The COM-B Model analyses what an individual requires to be able to make changes to their life, examining the behaviours and resources that the individuals has. A pregnant woman needs to have the psychological and physical capability to perform the change (West and Brown, 2013). This includes skills and tools to be able to stop smoking. Not all women need to have Nicotine replacement therapy to help them, but they need to have the knowledge how to stop. This is where the referral from the midwife to the NHS Stop Smoking Service can help (NHS, 2020).

In the passage above, there are seven sentences. Five begin with 'th' words.

Full stops, capital letters (and some commas) have been inserted, as appropriate, in the sentences below:

> As well as capability, the woman needs to have the social and physical opportunity. This includes giving the woman time to make the change, as smoking is an addiction.

> However, to make a change the woman needs to have the motivation to do this. This is where information shared between the woman and the midwife can potentially help the woman.

> I would often liaise with the social worker and other multidisciplinary teams to ensure that service users' issues were dealt with and resolved, therefore having a satisfactory outcome. This inspired me to become a social worker.

> This activity promotes creativity for children. Through this activity, children express new ideas and use resources to represent their ideas. Creativity helps children develop problem-solving abilities and think of solutions, using imagination and application of knowledge. Therefore, this activity promotes an outcome of value and worth through creativity, because the children accomplish a creative task, the work is praised, and they feel appreciated. Thus, the children were able to have their self-esteem and confidence boosted.

'Wh' words are link words and often follow commas. They do not start sentences, unless they are part of an introductory phrase or asking a question.

Commas have been placed in front of the 'wh' words where appropriate in the sentences below:

> I chose this because of the lapels, which are not featured on other patterns I found.

> A smaller part would be more appealing to the actor, who would then not have to memorise so many lines.

Introductory words include useful link words, like 'Therefore', 'Consequently', 'However' and 'Furthermore', which are always followed by a comma to separate them from the rest of the sentence.

Two of the three participants were able to form a strong connection to the deaf community and the use of sign language, whereas one participant struggled to identify with the deaf community and sign language, due to his late diagnosis.

The monochrome image used for Robert, with intertwined shapes running through it, represents his powerful and stern presence, whilst also representing that there is more going on in his life than first thought.

The linear, harsh lines of the geometric shapes represent the intimidating nature of the powerful, older characters, whilst the flowing, natural shapes and lines represent the feelings of romance, youthfulness and fun, encapsulating the socialite characters.

You can also have introductory phrases, which usually set the scene or give a detail. They are also separated from the rest of the sentence by a comma.

In the 1990 film version of *The Handmaid's Tale*, the costumes have changed from those described in the book, with* the handmaids not being as concealed as in the novel, where even their faces are hidden by a winged habit.

*Note the use of 'with' to link phrases as well as a 'wh' word.

The difference in size between the two flats could be down to many reasons: it could be because the first flat was constructed at a time when there was a large deficit in housing after the First World War, whereas the second flat was not.

After the four-week trial period is over, the researcher can suggest a time to meet up, when the participant can share with him the impact of the intervention.

Findings suggest that it is appearance training in conversations with friends that leads to changes in body dissatisfaction in girls, whereas for the boys, it was the internalization of body ideal that led to changes in body dissatisfaction (Carlson Jones, 2004).

The conduct of the President left many people feeling that the United States had reverted back to an old way of thinking, where women were objectified for sex appeal and were not equal to their male counterparts. This has a correlation with *The Handmaid's Tale*, when society has advanced but then regresses back to an older philosophy. (2)

And, finally…

20 Dos and Don'ts!

1. DO get to know the different Control + buttons. I only discovered Control + Z (Undo) recently, but it is invaluable when you suddenly manage to delete a section of your work! As if by magic, and to your massive relief, you can bring it back!

2. DO avoid using 'everyday' verbs when a more specific or academic one is available – or when one is not needed at all!

    e.g., **The author looks to review personality disorders to see if they are a western concept or "universal" from a cultural perspective.**

    This could be rewritten:

    The author reviews personality disorders to examine/establish/ investigate whether they are a western concept or "universal" from a cultural perspective.

    Similarly, people often write that a report 'looks at' some subject or other. It is more academic to say the report examines, studies or even scrutinises! DO make a friend of the synonyms feature, when you right click on a word to see alternative words you could use.

3. DO avoid bland words, like 'lots of'.

    Unfortunately, synonyms of 'lots' give rather cute, but not very academic alternatives, like 'oodles' and 'heaps'! Think of an alternative, like 'many', and then choose a synonym from the list of options.

    Tip: Don't use inverted commas around the word for which you want synonyms, or no results will appear!

4. DO use the 'Replace' feature at the top right-hand side of the ribbon in Word, when you need to correct a misspelling that recurs in your work or change a lower-case letter into an upper-case one. If you don't have it on your ribbon, select Control + H, and the Find and Replace box will appear.

    A student of mine changed 77 examples of 'Wembley park' in his dissertation to 'Wembley Park' at the click of a mouse, taking seconds instead of hours trawling through his work! In the next few seconds, he altered 44 'Wembley stadiums' to 'Wembley Stadiums'.

5. DO use capital letters for names, titles, places, etc. Where should they go in the sentence below about various train stations?

> Improvements in the Wembley area included a major refurbishment and extension to Wembley park station, modernisation of Wembley central and the new 'White horse bridge' linking Wembley stadium station with the stadium (Brent council, 2009).

The corrected version is here, with changes ==highlighted==.

> Improvements in the Wembley area included a major refurbishment and extension to Wembley ==Park== station, modernisation of Wembley ==Central== and the new 'White ==Horse Bridge==' linking Wembley ==Stadium== station with the stadium (Brent ==Council==, 2009).
>
> Brent Council. (2009). Wembley masterplan supplementary planning document [PDF]. https://www.Brent.gov.uk/media/333266/Wembley%20Masterplan.pdf.

Note that stations are a common noun, so are spelt with a lower case 's', but the titles that make them specific begin with a capital letter. Streets and roads are also commonplace, but a specific address, like Vernon Road or Church Street will use capital letters.

You could say that the White Horse Bridge should just have a small 'b' for 'bridge', but it is a well-known feature so is capitalised throughout. If in doubt, Google it, as I just did!

6. DO copy authors' names correctly for in-text citations. Tutors will know the relevant sources and there is no excuse for copying them wrongly! Several of the references given for student work in this book were spelt incorrectly, making it very difficult for me to double-check the reference.

7. When using the word 'impact', DO say whether it impacts negatively or positively, as everything has some kind of impact.

8. Don't say 'allow _for_' unless you are explaining, for example, that a dress is made one size bigger than needed to 'allow for' expansion! Generally, 'allow' means 'permit', whereas 'enable' is a stronger word, suggesting empowerment.

9. DO be consistent when using more than one 'ing' verb in a sentence. The following sentence is wrong. Why?

> Social work professionals have developed core values to improve service delivery, by dealing ethically with complex dilemmas, liaising effectively with multi-agencies, and reduce conflicts between needs and resources.

After using 'by dealing ethically with…', all the verbs that follow in the sentence need to be 'ing' verbs, or participles, as well:

> Social work professionals have developed core values to improve service delivery, by dealing ethically with complex dilemmas, liaising effectively with multi-agencies, and <u>reducing</u> conflicts between needs and resources.

10. When starting a new paragraph, DO use a short, introductory sentence. Longer sentences can follow. It is now generally accepted as good practice to have a range of sentence lengths and paragraph lengths in your writing.

11. When using a dash, DO have a space on either side of it. This differentiates it from a hyphen, which joins words and has NO space on either side (as in 'second-hand' and 'mother-in-law').

12. The word 'however' suggests a change of idea. Therefore, DO have a change of sentence, even if 'however' comes at the beginning, middle or end of the sentence:

    > However, another researcher thought differently.

    > Another researcher, however, thought differently.

    > Another researcher thought differently, however.

13. DON'T separate the subject of a sentence from its verb with a comma, as in the sentence below:

    > Another model of vacuum cleaner that has been brought out, is the Superclean 2020 model.

    The subject of the sentence is a long one – "Another model of vacuum cleaner that has been brought out…" – but that is absolutely fine. The verb that goes with the subject is "is".

    Keep the subject and its verb together, without a comma in between:

    > Another model of vacuum cleaner that has been brought out is the Superclean 2020 model.

    When I read work aloud, I often take a big breath when there is a comma between a subject and its verb, to show how it does not sound correct e.g., Susie (big breath) went shopping.

    Other examples:

    > The reason why I chose the Scarecrow Festival, was that it is accessible to a wide range of members in the local community. (Wrong! ☹)

> The reason why I chose the Scarecrow Festival was that it is accessible to a wide range of members in the local community. (Right! ☺)

14. DO look for the subject of a sentence and the verb that should be next to it, to help you separate the main sentence from the introductory phrase(s) with a comma, as in:

    > Due to Covid 19 restrictions at the time of research all studies had to be conducted via other methods.

    The subject of the sentence is 'all studies' and the accompanying verb is 'had to be conducted…' Thus, anything BEFORE the subject is detail or the introductory phrase and can be separated from the main sentence with a comma.

    > Due to Covid 19 restrictions at the time of research, all studies had to be conducted via other methods.

15. DO label tables and figures in numbers. Table 1. is written ABOVE the table, whereas Figure 2. is written BELOW the figure. Note that both are followed by a full stop, even if you go on to describe what is in the table or figure.

    Harvard referencing uses numbers for the Appendices, but in APA 7th referencing the Appendices use letters of the alphabet. If you have more than 26 appendices, you double the letter of the alphabet, so the 27th appendix is written Appendix AA. Note: The Appendices are written after the References list.

16. DON'T use contractions – where two words are squashed or 'contracted' into one, with an apostrophe showing where letters have thus been pushed out. This is not good practice in academic writing. Use the full term 'was not' rather than 'wasn't', for example.

17. DON'T use capital letters and full stops in bullet points that are words and phrases. It depends on the academic referencing style you use as to whether you use them with sentences or not. I find bullet-pointed sentences look better with capital letters and full stops.

18. DO set your spellchecker to English (United Kingdom) rather than English (United States), so that the spellchecker does not change your carefully spelt 'colour' to 'color'! You can do this through the Review section of the ribbon at the top of the Word screen, then select 'Language' on the Tool Bar below and choose English (United Kingdom).

19. DO put commas between dates when you use them. Separate the month from the year, and the day from the month with a comma. For example:

    The next meeting of the committee will take place on Monday, May 5th, 2021, at 7.30 p.m.

20. DO read through your work TWICE when finished. The first time, check the sense of what you have written and ensure it meets the learning objectives and assignment requirements. The second time, proofread it for punctuation, grammar, repetition of words and phrases etc. It is hard to check for meaning at the same time as punctuation! Different skills are required and are best applied separately.

CONGRATULATIONS!

You have now graduated as a competent proofreader!

Clare has been teaching from the tender age of four, when she set up a school for friends, giving them sums to compute and poems to compose! She gained an Honours degree in English at Durham University and later a Master's degree in Educational Studies at York St. John. After beginning her 'adult' teaching career in a primary school, she ran a unit for pupils with specific learning difficulties in a secondary school and then went on to work with dyslexic students in further and higher education. Her first book, **Spelling Made Magic**, distilled all the tips and tricks she had taught her younger pupils, while **Punctuation Matters!** is aimed at students from GCSE level through to university and beyond. Clare has two daughters and two granddaughters, and lives with her partner in West Yorkshire.